Beginning with Books

Beginning with Books

Library Programming for Infants, Toddlers, and Preschoolers

Nancy N. DeSalvo

Foreword by Faith Hektoen

Library Professional Publications   1993

© 1993 Nancy N. DeSalvo. All rights reserved.
First published in 1993 as a
Library Professional Publication, an imprint of
The Shoe String Press, Inc.
Hamden, Connecticut 06514

Library of Congress Cataloging-in-Publication Data

Beginning with books : library programming for
infants, toddlers, and preschoolers
by Nancy DeSalvo.
p.   cm.
1. Libraries, Children's—Activity programs.
2. Preschool children—Books and reading.
3. Toddlers—Books and reading.
4. Infants—Books and reading.   I. Title.
Z718.3.D48   1992   92-14858   027.62'5—dc20
ISBN 0-208-02318-6 (pbk.)

The paper used in this publication meets the
minimum requirements of American
National Standard for Information Sciences—
Permanence of Paper for Printed Library Materials.
ANSI   Z39.48-1984.⊗

Printed in the United States of America

✻ Contents ─────────────

Of all the 'props' of childhood,
none are more compelling or conducive
to make-believe and fantasy than
the books children read or hear read
to them by a warm, loving adult.

The House of Make-Believe
Dorothy G. and Jerome L. Singer

☙ Foreword ─────────────────────

Child development research from the 1970s onward has shown us how young children respond to stimulation by and interaction with language and language-related activities. We know, too, that a close relationship exists between a child's interest in reading and early language experiences, adult involvement, play activities, and reading aloud. When these factors are put together in an intelligent, structured, and caring way, they can serve as the basis for early childhood programs which will help to meet the needs of caregivers and parents, children, and in a larger sense, the community and even the nation as well.

Young parents and parents of young children have a real appetite for information about the intellectual and physical development, health, nutrition, and safety of their children. They need to know what materials to use with their babies and toddlers, how and when to use them, and what needs and purposes they serve. The wise librarian therefore understands that programs for young children really are parent programs, too, and makes sure that they highlight the parent's role and demonstrate ways for parents to share books, toys, music, and movement with their children.

The idea of library programming for infants, toddlers, preschoolers, and their parents or caregivers is taking hold across the country. But many librarians, in spite of good will, are not sure how and where to begin in offering meaningful activities that will satisfy a child's needs developmentally, keep parents interested and enthusiastic, and promote the social concerns of the library. What they need is an action plan that can be used, or used as a model, for a program in their own community. That is what this book offers.

Beginning with Books is firmly rooted in particular concerns about children and larger concerns about society. In 1970, the White House Conference on Children brought national attention to the plight of families raising children in a technological world. Now that we are into the last decade of this century, we see even greater changes in our society that make for greater challenges. There is the impact on children of the massive changes in family life and structure; the growing number of single and teenage parent families; the high ratio of children in poverty, or homeless; the rising death rate for the young; problems in literacy and education; the harsh realities of the national economy; and startling changes throughout the world's population. At this time, when it is most important for public institutions to take a major role in the welfare of our children, funds and jobs are being cut.

It is therefore incumbent upon us to be as clear in our goals and as effective in our methods of reaching children, and their parents, as possible. The best way to begin is at the beginning, and this book provides a map.

FAITH HEKTOEN

🦋 Preface ———————————————

This book is a direct outgrowth of my experience first as a children's librarian, and later as Coordinator of Children's and Young Adult Services since 1974 in the Farmington, Connecticut Public Library.

Farmington, a residential suburb in the Hartford metropolitan area, has retained its distinctive character through maintenance of its historic district and careful land use planning for the future. Most of Farmington's residents are professionals or executives in the area's insurance, financial, or industrial companies—well-educated and highly motivated parents where children are concerned. Our population is multilingual and multicultural, too, due to the many foreign students from China, India, Japan, and Europe, who come with their families to study at the two colleges and universities in the area.

Because we are dedicated to working with parents of very young children, and because we see an early start with books as an early lease on life, we try to serve the needs of *all* members of the community in our in-house and outreach programs. Single parents and teenage parents are especially targeted, due to their critical needs for encouragement and support.

Although the programs given in this book were originally designed for use in the Farmington Library, they are as universal as can be in their application to other populations. Babies, after all, require the simplest, most basic kinds of interaction—and can only benefit from the sights, sounds, touch, rhythm, rocking, and play this book offers. Parents, whether already knowledgeable about child development or not, can learn the literature that appeals to young children at different stages of life, and become familiar with the songs, films, and toys that reinforce good literature experiences. What better function can a public

xii   Preface

library perform than to bring to parent and child alike a warm, close experience with each other, and with books?

First, I would like to thank Faith Hektoen, the Children's Consultant at the Connecticut State Library from 1967–1988, who provided the training and workshops that gave me the background to do these programs. She was the inspiration who sparked children's librarians in Connecticut to formulate higher goals and strive for excellence. She helped me with the early manuscript and made many suggestions throughout the writing of this book. Also, I would like to thank my son, Andy, who has a great deal of patience and helped me with the important job of getting started, and my sister, Cynthia Neal, former Chief of Children's and Branch Services at the Providence Public Library, who read my early manuscript and made suggestions. Some of the ideas in the book she had initiated in Rhode Island.

I would like to thank my staff in the children's room, Patricia LeBouthillier, Lucille O'Connell, Peter Guglietta, Jane Farley and Patricia Morgen, who consistently back me up in my philosophy of children's services and are always willing to go the extra mile to make for one of the busiest and best children's rooms in Connecticut.

I would also like to thank Lucille O'Connell who typed my manuscript and had to deal with my handwriting, as well as my daughter-in-law, Cindy, who put the manuscript on computer.

I would like to thank my children, Bill, Bart, Chris, Missy, Andy and Sally who loved good books and provided me with the hands-on training which later proved invaluable to me in my work. It would be appropriate at this time to note that it was my mother who read aloud to her children by the hour and introduced to us the very best in children's literature.

With special thanks to my husband, Ben, who had to deal with the frustrations and temperament of a first-time author, and Mildred Whitney, my volunteer in the children's room for the last twenty-three years, who is a wonderful sounding board.

Lastly, I want to thank my editor, Diantha Thorpe, who took over the editing of this book and had to deal with an inexperienced author and had endless patience and wonderful suggestions.

1 _____

Why We Need Preschool Programs

Many parents have less time to spend with their preschool children than they did twenty years ago, as the number of families where both parents work and the number of single-parent households have steadily increased. Parents wish to make time with their children as rewarding and instructive as possible, but are uncertain what the best activities are for this. For their part, children need to enlarge their experiences, build their understanding of the world, experiment with language, and acquire the story sense that will help in developing reading skills—all before going to school at age five or six. A preschool child also needs to learn the interactive skills that come from belonging to a group, such as a nursery school or daycare community.

The public library is one place where these concerns are being addressed today. Librarians, realizing that successful reading is related closely to very early childhood exposure to books and language, are pushing to broaden the public library's role in helping parents and other caregivers. A public library with *comprehensive* service for preschool children can be very valuable to parents who hope to develop their child's language and reading skills. First, the library can provide sound books on child development and assist the parents in selecting appropriate books, tapes, toys, and records for their individual child. Second, the library can organize *programs* for preschoolers and their parents—for demonstration and participation are the most effective way of introducing these library materials in *creative ways*. The library preschool program gives the parent a chance to observe the child's response to different stimuli and to clearly understand the importance of play. In fact, a well-designed program has an effect that goes far beyond the time the child spends in the library because it gives the parent constructive ideas to repeat or further develop at home.

This book focuses on such creative library programming for the preschool child. The materials, bibliographies, and programs offered here are ones that I have tested and used successfully in the Farmington, Connecticut Public Library for the past fourteen years. Although this book is for librarians who need ideas, information and encouragement for doing preschool programming, daycare and nursery school teachers and parents will also find the lists of materials and the descriptions of the different programs of great value.

Many forces are at work in society today that must be considered by all librarians who seek to serve preschoolers and parents. On one hand many women are giving birth at a later age, as many are working and establishing careers, thus marrying later and having children later. As Margaret M. Clark, a professor in educational psychology at the University of Strathclyde, England, states in the book *Young Fluent Readers*, these women tend to have a tremendous interest in their children's development. In fact the age of mothers of fluent child readers was found to be much higher than average (p. 41). In my own experience I've found that these mothers tend to demand more from libraries than younger mothers do.

More is known now about the capacity of infants and preschoolers to learn. Burton White, author of *The First Three Years* and director and principal investigator of the famed Harvard University preschool project, and now Director of the Center for

Parent Education, Newton, Massachusetts, states in "Baby Research Comes of Age" that the "emphasis on education spawned by the Head Start movement is the most dramatic change in our approach to the studies of infancy. Not only did Head Start provide a *raison d'être* for studies in infancy, but once middle class parents caught on to the likely significance of learning in the pre-school years there was no holding them back" (p. 46).

These parents too are actively approaching the libraries for help in child rearing. Our ideas about what children need in order to learn successfully are changing as well. According to Tiffany Field, Professor of Pediatrics, Psychology, and Psychiatry at the University of Miami School of Medicine, in the same article, "the study of infancy is in its early childhood, and what we have learned has contributed to significant differences in the rearing of infants. Now they are treated as interesting, sophisticated and impressionable human beings with minds of their own that need careful nurturing and enrichment" (p. 47). Field gives an example of nurturing in her book *Infancy,* one of the books from the developing child series published by Harvard University Press. She describes infant exploration and play:

> By six or seven months the infant is usually capable of locomotion and shows his autonomy by crawling away from the parent to explore the environment. At first the infant will remain within close range of the parent, but as locomotion develops and as exploratory appetite increases it moves farther away, remaining separated from the parent for longer periods of time. In a number of experiments it has become clear that when the infant is playing with the mother or father present, the infant will move away and explore the environment voluntarily. However, if the parents are absent, the infant's exploration of the environment is greatly decreased. (p. 56)

As I will show in this book, the children's librarian can be effective in enhancing parents' capabilities for building rich experiences in reading, talking, and enjoying language with their children. However, we must also be aware of unrealistic parental expectations. Unfortunately, many parents pressure children's librarians to help teach their children to read at an early age. This clearly is not our role, and may also do definite harm to children not yet ready to read. Many parents, too, are more interested in teaching their children certain concepts, such as numbers, letters, and colors, than in teaching the enjoyment of books. Dr. Burton White and Dr. Michael K. Meyerhoff in "Making the Grade as Parents," summarize their ideas this way:

> First, you are likely to make the greatest differences in the academic prospects of young children if you reach them during the first three years, when the foundations for later development are laid. Furthermore, the most inexpensive and efficient method is to work through the people who have the greatest influence on children's lives during this period—their parents. Finally, most parents, regardless of social status, educational level or cultural background, are eager to receive the information and support they need to be effective in their role as their children's first and most important teachers. (p. 38)

Thus parents themselves are a natural and valuable "resource" for programming, as well as a potential "market" for it, and the library certainly can be an ideal institution to lead them. With that the case, the librarian should also take the initiative to seek out those parents who wouldn't normally come into the library— such as single parents, unwed mothers, and educationally or otherwise deprived parents of preschoolers. For if some parents are older now, some are much younger. There is a dramatic increase in the number of teenage mothers, many of whom are poorly educated and living in economic uncertainty.

All public institutions should be aware of the plight of the nation's children and should be willing, indeed eager, to help them acquire needed learning skills. In "A Promise at Risk," Susan Champlin Taylor expressed this concern:

> Looking at children as America's prospective workers, parents, voters, and taxpayers, it becomes a frightening prospect to realize that one in five of them, 13 million children in all, live in poverty; that 12 million have no health insurance coverage and often go without medical care; that one-fourth of all teenagers drop out of high school; that countless thousands more will graduate with reading, writing and reasoning skills inadequate for the job market; and that nearly half a million teenage girls will become mothers this year, virtually guaranteeing a continuation in the cycle of poverty. (p. 32)

We must stop this cycle. Education is the key. One out of six babies born in the United States today is the child of a teenage mother; 96% of these girls keep their babies. These mothers, especially, need a great deal of help not just in raising their children but in coping with their situation.

Social service groups and government agencies recognize this snowballing social catastrophe. Marian Wright Edelman, President of the Children's Defense Fund, has said: "We have to make a critical mass of Americans understand that the breakdown of the American family is a great threat, greater than the savings-and-loan crisis" (Taylor, p. 84). Scott Fosler from the Committee for Economic Development believes that parents should be the motivators and he compares today's families with poor families who survived the Depression of the 30s. "Their families were very poor but they worked hard and made it," says Fosler. "Looking at the children of today they wondered why they couldn't overcome their obstacles. What they came to understand is that the key is not just whether a family is poor, it's whether the kids are getting the kind of parenting that can provide them with the support and nurturing and the motivation to overcome those obstacles. Today so many kids who are poor are not getting that kind of parenting. In many cases there's only one parent, usually a mother with limited education, often a teenager herself, struggling to make ends meet. It's very difficult for kids in that situation to break out" (Taylor, p. 39).

Robert Keeshan (better known as Captain Kangaroo) reiterated this position in his book, *Growing Up Happy*. The purpose of his book, Keeshan says, is to help parents nurture:

> Childhood must be a time for a child to learn about the world, to love, to enjoy being loved, to satisfy curiosity, to gain confidence and develop self-esteem. These activities are critical to the natural rhythm of development. To rush it is like asking a musician to play Beethoven's "Choral" symphony in double time; it's not very pleasant to the ears. Life's rhythms are carefully planned, and a parent is like a symphony conductor, trying to lead the many facets of a child's personality, uniting them in a pleasing way. The parent/conductor must be careful to respect the music as written. Rushing it will bring very undesirable results. (p. 212)

THE FOUNDATIONS OF PROGRAMMING

The 1970 White House Conference on Children brought national emphasis to the lack of parent support services and the increasing stress of bringing up children in a technological society. It was found at this conference that young parents, and parents with young children, have great needs for information about child development, health, nutrition, safety, and intellectual stimulation; and for materials to use with young children, how and when to use them, for what purposes, emotional needs, and so on. These needs are addressed by types of parent support services in libraries, often with the help of community resource specialists.

In Connecticut the White House Conference led to a series of workshops called "The Pilot Project in Early Childhood Education." This project was offered in 1972 by the Connecticut State Library's Division of Public Library Services through the children's consultant, Faith H. Hektoen. It enrolled twenty-five nursery school or daycare heads and interested parents in learning sessions developed at St. Joseph's College in West Hartford, Connecticut in consultation with the Connecticut State Department of Education. This program was followed in 1974 by a graduate institute, "The Development of Young Children and the Public Library Today," which provided the background for Farmington's "Terrific Two's" program started in January 1977. This parent-child program is detailed here in chapter 4. It, and other parent support services, were justified by research carried out in Connecticut the following year.

This was a survey that measured and recorded daily use of public library children's services in fourteen public libraries from communities representing a broad cross section of society. It provided participating librarians with management information that improved the quality of library service. The program was conducted by Faith Hektoen and was written up in the *School Library Journal* in April, 1980. In the Farmington Library, for example, in November 1978 we had 189 reference questions: fifteen requests for early childhood records; seven requests for toys; twenty-two questions about books for the young child (two and under); and twenty-five requests for books from the parent/ teacher shelf. These sixty-nine requests, out of a total of 189, showed us that more than one-third of all questions asked related to parenting and young children.

Additional documentation alerted us to the number of patron questions about the "Terrific Two's" program. In a typical morning an average of ten inquiries about the program was received. This interest led to more programming for infants and parents, toddlers and parents, and parents alone, about topics concerning their children.

In the last ten years the Connecticut State Library Division of Library Development has offered librarians two excellent seminar series on working with very young children. The first of these was a Library Services Construction Act (LSCA) funded seminar series called "Beginnings: Public Library Services for Two-Year-Olds and Their Parents." The need for this training session came out of the very successful "Terrific Two's" program run in Farmington, which was reported on at the American Library Association (ALA) annual meeting in June 1977, where it generated much interest.

Word of the Farmington "Terrific Two's" had spread throughout the state. Many parents whose older children were involved with preschool story hour wanted library programs for their two-year-olds. It might be expected that any vigorous person who enjoys two-year-olds and who has had experiences in library story hours could successfully manage such programming, but this was not always the case. Many children's librarians had very little background in child development.

"Beginnings" was the solution. It was described in the manual written by program director Frank Self: " 'Beginnings' is a parenting program to help parents with their very young children. It helps parents develop their skills in playing with their very young children." Self went on to explain that "to facilitate this parenting program, children's librarians must also extend their ideas about the development of very young children, about library programs involving very young children, and also about their role vis-a-vis children and parents in those programs."

To achieve the overall purpose, training seminars were held for children's librarians in fall 1979 and winter 1980 and Dr. Self wrote a manual of basic information necessary to develop and implement such library programs. There were sixty-six people trained in three different seminars. Each seminar had four sessions, and a follow-up session, involving all the participants, was held in May 1980. As a result, thirty-five library two-year-old programs followed the next year. A second program was held in fall 1984 to train a new group. Again, this was a LSCA-funded series and ran for five all-day sessions. It was entitled "Services for Up-to-Three's and Their Parents," and again was coordinated by Faith Hektoen and early childhood consultants for the Connecticut Department of Education. By now parents were asking for help and programs for children younger than two so the purpose of this second series was to help children's librarians evaluate the needs and abilities of infants and toddlers, together with their parents' specific informational needs. It also suggested enriching experiences that parents could develop further at home with their children.

The series was carefully planned to offer practical help, some specific background knowledge, and some opportunity for interaction. Leaders in the field were brought in as speakers. The following topics were addressed in this seminar series:

- What up-to-three's are like
- What do their parents need?
- What options do parents have for child care?
- Play: helping parents understand its importance for infants and toddlers
- Hands-on with toys (replicating toys, found objects also)
- Early language
- Books for infants and toddlers
- Criteria for selecting books
- Cooperation, networking activities

- Family focus programming
- Infant programming
- Parent support materials—the vertical file resource
- Dealing with library problems serving up-to-three's
- Young parent programs
- Services for teenage parents

Among the important information shared at both seminars were criteria for evaluating books. Three criteria, more reliable than such commonly used ones as selection based on author's and illustrator's reputation, were cited:

1. Ease of focus of attention vs. distraction and diffusion of attention.
2. Semantic clarity of illustrations and text vs. lack of clarity.
3. Familiarity of subjects and language vs. foreignness of subjects and language.

Librarians learned that even established authors can err in choosing age-suitable material for toddlers. Also, that the beautiful artwork of many talented illustrators can be lost on young children, whose visual comprehension is not developed enough to relate to it. Older picture books, such as Don Freeman's *Corduroy*, were easier to evaluate as children's librarians were more familiar with what this age group likes and understands and they receive instant feedback from the children whether they like the book or not. This is not true with younger children who often only respond positively to the book after the parent has read it several times at home.

To run successful programs for children under three, the children's librarians must be able to evaluate materials on an individual basis. Even lists by experienced librarians can be misleading. Unfortunately, this is very time consuming, and the market is drenched with books for this age group, most of inferior quality. Even good books carefully evaluated can be a poor selection if assigned to a child of the wrong age.

Much of what is to follow in subsequent chapters of this book is an outgrowth of these early starts, burnished by actual experience, repetition, and re-evaluation in the library.

SELECTED "EARLY STARTS" FROM OTHER AREAS

The New York Public Library was an instigator in an interesting early childhood program. Under the leadership of Barbara Rollock, Coordinator of Children's Services in 1978, an Early Childhood Resource and Information Center (ERIC) was set up in a branch library. The Center is divided into two parts—the "Family Room" on one side and the "Program Room" on the other side—with shelves of resource books between the two areas. In the Family Room the preschoolers interact with toys (including housekeeping units), with their parents, and with other parents and children. They can drop in anytime when the Center is open. It makes a nice "getaway" place, especially for parents who are new in the area and for parents who live where there are no other families with small children.

The Center also provides workshops, mostly conducted by early childhood specialists, on many topics. Some of the subjects they cover are detection of learning problems, discipline, toy selection, music and movement, and book selection for the very young child. The workshops are very popular and require advance registration.

Another very interesting program for children's librarians was a course in early childhood education co-sponsored by New York University and the New York Public Library branch libraries in 1987. Conducted by well-known librarian and educator Ellin Peterson Greene, and funded by a Carnegie Foundation grant, it was designed to prepare librarians to meet the needs of individual branch neighborhoods for library services to preschool children, their parents, and caregivers. There were fifteen sessions. Goals and objectives of the course were:

1. To familiarize students with current research in early childhood and its implications for library service to young children and their caregivers.

2. To familiarize students with the history of library service to early childhood and various models of service with emphasis on the Early Childhood Resource and Information Center (ERIC) model.

3. To familiarize students with the developmental characteristics of children from birth through age five.

4. To familiarize students with print and nonprint materials appropriate for young children or their caregivers, the criteria for selection of materials, and guidelines for their use.

5. To develop students' expertise in storytelling, reading aloud, and other strategies for nurturing early interaction with stories and print.

6. To familiarize students with socioeconomic conditions, ethnicity, and family culture which affect library service for young children.

7. To develop students' expertise in interacting with parents and community agencies.

8. To develop students' expertise in administration of library service to early childhood, planning and publicity, staff training, recruitment and training of volunteers.

9. To assist students in designing and implementing model programs in early childhood for their branch community.

In Texas, Dr. Frances A. Smardo of the Dallas Public Library is a great advocate of preschool programming. One of the most interesting studies that she directed was a cooperative project of the Dallas Public Library and North Texas State University. The primary purpose of the study was to determine the most effective of three types of public library story hour programs for the acquisition of receptive language of preschool children of varying socioeconomic levels. Dr. Smardo concluded that:

- Live and film story hours are significantly more effective than no story hours.
- Live story hours are significantly more effective than video story hours.

- Story hours ranked in this decreasing order of effectiveness: live, film, video, and control (which was no story hour at all).

This is an effective study to cite when your director or board wonders why you are doing so many story hours or why you place so much importance on them.

At the 1978 ALA conference, Dr. Smardo gave out a series of recommendations regarding the role of the public library in serving young children from infancy to six years of age. Some of the most pertinent ones about programming are:

1. Children's librarians should be specifically prepared for work with adults and young children.

2. Children's librarians should have knowledge and expertise in children's literature, child development, and material selection for very young children.

3. Programs and services should be provided to permit parent-child interaction.

At this time, when the thrust of programming has settled on the 0–3 age range, it is important for the children's librarian to possess many qualifications. These are listed by Dr. Smardo in an article, "Are Librarians Prepared to Serve Young Children?" Some of these qualifications are:

1. An understanding of child development. (How many library schools require or offer courses in child development?)

2. The ability to work with parents. (Many children's librarians unfortunately back away from dealing with parents and thus do little or no parent programming).

3. The ability to relate not only to children's literature but to the literature of child psychology. (It is important to have a parent-teacher collection in the children's room so that staff can quickly get books to meet the needs of the parents). (p. 274–84)

The Orlando Public Library in Florida was one of the first library systems to get involved with infant programming. The library distributed a "B is for Baby" bibliography and a pamphlet for parents of newborns called "Catch 'em in the Cradle" in the maternity wards in eight different hospitals in Orlando. The library system also produced the film, *What's So Great About Books?* This film is 15 minutes long and is great for parent programs as it leads to some healthy discussions—among them, the use of TV, and reading to children long after they can read themselves. The age range of children in the film is such that you can show it to parents of newborns, but also to parents of children from kindergarten on up.

We need good preschool programs in our libraries, our daycare centers, and our nursery schools. Those that are to follow here draw on not just the efforts of pioneering librarians or child development researchers, but on the hands-on experience of the working librarian, the caregiver, and the teacher. And we should never ignore the contributions of children themselves! They have taught us much, and if we continue to regard them openly and honestly, to trust the validity of their reactions and take their likes and dislikes seriously, we will certainly enrich our childhood programs further. To begin, then, we can ask ourselves a few general questions about our programs:

- Do we provide an environment in which children are physically and emotionally comfortable?
- Do we provide a rich language environment that features verbal dialogue, not monologue?
- Do we promote opportunities for children to build self-confidence?
- Do we provide opportunities for children to improve their social skills?
- Do we provide a learning environment in which children are often free to move around and manipulate objects?
- Do we recognize that all children move through distinct stages of cognitive development?

- Do we recognize that all children, even those who are highly motivated, have plateaus in their cognitive learning?
- And last: do we provide opportunities for children to progress in all areas—cognitive, social, language, motor and self-help—at all stages of their development?

These thoughts can serve as guidelines in constructing programs for children in any town or city. Let us always keep them in mind.

2

Infant Programs Are Parent Programs

Parents of infants are looking for support. Though constantly bombarded with advice from thousands of "experts," they need to know how to choose what is right for their child. All infants need a caring person who cuddles and plays with them during the first year to insure healthy social development. While many parents normally respond to their children in a natural way, others need help in interacting with their child—whether by talking, singing, doing fingerplays, experiencing music, reading books or playing. All parents need help with selecting materials: they need to know why certain materials are more appropriate than others. They especially need the opportunity to discuss the behavior of their babies with other people having similar experiences. They need someone to defuse the academic push to force concepts on children before they are ready. They need assurance that it doesn't matter at what age a child learns to read; they need to know what *does* matter is how much he enjoys listening and looking and, later, reading himself. The children's librarian, in the non-threatening atmosphere of a public library, can be the one to provide these important parent support services.

FIRST STEPS INTO PROGRAMMING

Infant programs are parent programs, and a good way to begin implementing one is with a parent-infant kit. This kit is an introduction both to library resources and to appropriate activities for infants. Each one could contain books for the parent to use such as *Finger Plays* by Emilie Pouisson; *The First Three Years of Life* by Burton L. White; *The Baby Exercise Book* by Janine Levy; or *Reading and Loving* by Leila Berg. Include too a sample of a cloth book for baby, a toy, and a folder of resource lists. These lists should be a straightforward "map" of these materials available in the library: 1) books for parents; 2) records and toys to use with infants; 3) books for the very young; 4) books to give as presents; and 5) cloth books and board books. They should also contain a description of the films to be used in parent programming, which will be discussed later in this book. Experience has shown that these kits will prove to be very popular with young parents who are regular patrons of the library, but you still need to reach out into the community to draw attention to the program and the many materials for infants and toddlers in the children's department.

One way to do this is to distribute infant information packets to *all* new parents of babies born after a date of your choosing. Check the local newspaper for birth announcements and send a flyer inviting new parents to come into the library to pick up their packets. At the same time, encourage them to bring a photograph of their baby for display in the children's room, and use their coming in as an opportunity to give them an introductory tour of the whole library.

The infant information packet itself should be designed to give parents help and guidance in choosing and using materials with their child from birth to age one. You may need to enlist financial help with this project, and your Friends of the Library group is a good place to start. There may also be other resources—community groups such as school support organizations—or even child-related businesses such as book or toy stores, that could help. Perhaps you could win a grant from a philanthropic group. In any case, funding will depend on the rules governing your individual library and your own ability to make the necessary contacts.

A good assembly of materials for the infant information packet could be

1. A book—either gift book for the parent or board book for the child.

2. A brochure about children's services in the library.

3. A description of the Friends group (or other group) which funded the project.

4. A booklet containing the same resource lists cited earlier.

5. Information on the early developmental stages of infancy.

6. Information on developing speaking, reading, and later, writing skills with the growing child.

7. "New Baby Books." This is a list of books to help older siblings adjust to the new baby. See Appendix 1 for forty-five titles to choose from.

These efforts will bear the best and most fruit, however, if the parents are given support to implement the resources success-fully, and for this, actual programs are the answer. Some libraries do provide an informal get-together for parents and infants to meet other parents, to see some toys or fingerplays, and perhaps to sing a song. This kind of activity *does* bring parents to the library and gives them the opportunity to make friends and form play groups, and it is much better than nothing at all. But a structured program, one requiring registration and careful plan-ning of how materials are introduced to the parent for later use is, by far, the best approach.

When infants and parents cement an early bonding relation-ship with reading and the public library, children's reading interests develop faster than they do at the later preschool age programs. In our library programs, too, we have found that when a parent is part of the program, he or she becomes hooked on library service much more readily than when he or she leaves the child at the story hour and retires to another part of the library. Often the parents become interested in total library service. They use resources more frequently in the adult department and volunteer for the Friends of the Library and library committees. These parents are very vocal in publicizing the library in the community.

At first many parents are skeptical of actually coming to an infant program. It will take a number of sessions of hands-on use of the materials to instruct parents in how and what they can do. They need to see for themselves very simple things: that children should be able to focus on the objects in the books presented to them; that there should be no distracting background to confuse the child; and that figures should be clear. The child also needs to have books to identify with—ones containing such familiar subjects as animals and children— where illustrations relate directly and closely to the subject matter. Hopefully, after a few sessions the parents will soon be able to start evaluating materials themselves.

Parents can be encouraged to use music with their children. It is good for both the infant and parent. Often a new mother is very tense and tired, and singing to a child or playing music relaxes both mother and child, especially at bedtime or nap time while the child is being rocked. Parents can learn to put on a record or tape, or croon a lullaby to the baby. Using chants, fingerplays, rhymes, and songs from such as *Your Baby Needs Music* by Barbara Cass-Beggs, is the best way to help caregivers overcome self-consciousness. Music should be a staple of the parent program.

Another relaxing and informative component of the program is the use of magazine articles on child development and parental problems. These can be referred to and discussed. Good magazines for this purpose are *American Baby, Child, Children Today, Language Arts, Mothering, Pre-K, Reading Teacher, Totline,* and *Young Children.* Check your periodical resources for these, and if they are not there, encourage your library to order them. This draws other areas of the library, too, into what you are doing, just as the reference department could help with questions about child development. Naturally librarians are not experts in this area, but parents do ask questions about their children that cannot be answered on the spot. A good way to handle these queries is to take the week between sessions of your program and have the reference department assist in finding the answer for the inquiring parent.

DEVELOPMENTAL BASIS
FOR THE INFANT PROGRAM

The following resources for planning programs are very helpful. First is Ann Carlson's book, *Early Childhood Literature Sharing Programs in Libraries.* Carlson has developed a schema which is a compilation of early childhood development information from birth to three years of age with literature-sharing implications for library programs.

Children's librarians who may not have had a recent course in child development and who want to do infant programs, should find this outline very helpful. She does warn that although library programs are usually structured to the chronological age range of children, the literature-sharing activities should be based on the child's developmental level.

She divides the programs up into the following age ranges:

1. Birth to six months of age

2. Seven months to fourteen months of age

3. Fifteen months to twenty-four months of age

4. Twenty-five months to thirty-six months of age.

For infants we concentrate on the first two parts, taking the child up to fourteen months. Carlson divides the developmental information for birth to six months of age into the following exploratory behaviors. I have given shortened explanations of each, but for more depth, see pages 24–31 of her book.

1. VISUAL EXPLORATION. Infants start to recognize familiar objects such as their bottles. They respond to people and especially like faces. At first, babies are more attracted to high-contrast patterns than to color or brightness. They start to see in color at about four months of age.

2. TACTILE EXPLORATION. Babies start to explore with their hands. They want to grasp and shake objects and touch people.

3. ORAL EXPLORATION. Everything that babies can pick up goes into their mouths. They are starting to teethe, so they especially like objects that relieve the soreness of their gums.

4. EXPLORATION BY LISTENING. Infants respond more and more to the human voice. Babies love faces and love to hear sound coming from them.

5. DEVELOPMENT OF TRUST AND DEPENDENCY. Infants have a growing sense of belonging and relate to the consistent care of the caregiver. They start to depend upon the caring person.

This early childhood development information leads to the following possibilities for literature-sharing:

1. Talking and singing to the newborn infant (especially by the parent) should stress lullabies. If the parent can't sing very well, there are some super lullaby and early childhood song records, such as:

   Lullabies and Laughter with the Lullaby Lady by Pat Carfra
   Ella Jenkins's Nursery Rhymes by Ella Jenkins
   Activity Songs for Kids by Marcia Berman
   Songs to Grow On by Woody Guthrie

2. Place large clear pictures in the infant environment. Some of these clear pictures could be cut out of magazines. Put inexpensive see-through contact paper on them so they will last, and place them where the infant can see them.

3. Begin to show a variety of picture books to the infant, making sure there is good figure-ground contrast against a

solid color background. Good examples are the Brimax Books object lesson series. The objects are outlined in black and are very clear to the child. Some titles are *A First Book*, *In My Kitchen*, *In My Nursery*, *In My Garden*, and *In My Toybox*.

For the second stage, seven months to fourteen months, Ann Carlson lists the following development information which is simplified here for each category:

1. LANGUAGE DEVELOPMENT: SOUNDS. The child tries to imitate all kinds of sounds and tries new words.

2. LANGUAGE DEVELOPMENT: SENTENCES. The child will begin to understand simple commands and start to obey the caregiver.

3. LEARNING NAMES OF OBJECTS. The child tries to make the sound for familiar objects such as cup or ball, etc.

4. DEVELOPMENT OF EVOCATIVE MEMORY. The child starts to remember things. He doesn't have to see the ball if it has rolled under the couch but remembers that the ball went there. He starts to remember events for longer periods of time.

5. DEVELOPMENT OF RECOGNITION OF MOTHER AND FATHER. The child becomes very attached to parents or caregivers. Some will cry when they encounter strangers.

6. DEVELOPMENT OF CURIOSITY. Children begin to crawl and explore their environments. They want to handle everything they come in contact with.

This early childhood development information leads to the following possibilities for literature-sharing:

1. Keep singing and talking to the child. Language becomes very important to them. Use nursery rhymes and rhythm books and do fingerplays with them.

2. The child becomes very interested in objects. Use toys or other objects to show them the relationship of the two-

dimensional pictures in the book with the three-dimensional real objects.
3. Read and reread their favorite books. Repetition and familiarity are essential at this age.

Parents and children's librarians are very interested in very young children's book-handling behaviors. In the book, *More Than the ABC's: Early Stages of Reading and Writing*, Judith A. Schickedanz lists on page 12 the different behaviors you are likely to observe. Some of them are:

1. Makes eye contact with the pictures, but without hand contact (2–4 months).
2. Grasps the book with hands and brings it up to the mouth to suck and chew; shakes, crumples, and waves the book (5–10 months).
3. Deliberately tears paper pages, if offered (5–15 months).
4. Helps an adult reader turn the pages (7–8 months).
5. Gives the book to an adult to read (8–10 months).

Schickedanz sums up early book behaviors by stating that young children are very different. Some babies between the ages of five and ten months literally devour books, while other babies are content to look at books without taking them in hand and mouth. The librarian or parent should watch the baby and try to adjust experiences and interactions to match *what the baby can, and likes, to do.*

Another practical resource for parent-infant programs is a twenty-five minute videocassette and pamphlet produced by the American Library Association in 1986. It is titled *Sharing Books with Young Children*, with Betsy Hearne, and that is exactly what Hearne does: she shows you what books to use and how to use them. As she says in the film:

There is nothing that speaks stronger for books than the experience of reading them. The first years of a child's life are the best time for that experience to begin. Reading is a *physical* and *emotional* experience long before its an intellectual one. Young children need to chew on books, hug books, laugh at them, touch and feel them and associate them with a warm voice and an interested adult. Then, by the time they are confronted with books as a test of their reading capabilities, they will trust in the pleasure that stories and art bring as the ultimate reward. Books have become friends instead of enemies.

PHYSICAL SPACE FOR THE PROGRAM

It is very important that the library provide a good setting for the infant program. The babies should be able to crawl around and explore their environment. A good learning environment encourages infant exploration.

Jean Piaget, the noted Swiss psychologist who is recognized as a pioneer in the investigation of the origin and development of children's intellectual faculties, was among the first to emphasize that the most basic cognitive processes depend on infant active exploration of the environment. Also, he stressed the importance of variety in the development of early exploratory behavior. In "Infant Exploratory Play," David A. Caruso, who received his doctorate in human development and family studies at Cornell University as a child care specialist, outlines several goals which librarians or daycare center staff can use in developing social environments that encourage exploratory play. These suggestions can also be followed through at home with the parent and child:

1. Allow each infant ample opportunity for self-initiated exploratory play, both with objects and people.
2. Be aware of, and respond positively and in a variety of ways to, each infant's self-initiated interpersonal exploration.
3. Encourage more passive infants to explore by initiating play and then passing the leading role over to the child as much as possible.

A carpeted room offers a safe and warm environment for play. If you do not have a small room to run children's programs in, then block off an area of a larger room with chairs to make a small, inviting place. The babies are not old enough to do much running around so they will crawl around in the designated area. The parents can sit on chairs or on the floor with their babies. Most of them will gravitate to the floor. Suggest that they arrange themselves in a semi-circle facing you and the tables on which you have the materials to share with them.

At home many parents like to use a playpen for their infants. This rates high for safety but you can encourage them to childproof a room at home to let their little ones explore. Make sure that they understand clearly that they *must* be present and watch their baby carefully. Infants of this age can move with great speed and their ability to get into trouble quickly cannot be underestimated.

STRUCTURE OF THE PROGRAM SERIES

Plan a series of seven sessions for your program. The first one should be in the evening and is for the parents alone. This is an orientation meeting to explain what will happen in the infant series.

I find that I can cover most of the pertinent material in six sessions plus the orientation. The program is geared mostly toward the parent although the infants truly enjoy the music and the toys, the books somewhat, and seeing other babies and parents. My programs last one hour. Other librarians might want to schedule 30 minutes and conduct more sessions. I do not limit enrollment for infant programs (although it has never gone over twenty-five). Babies are less active than toddlers and two-year-olds (which programs I do limit to twelve). I usually schedule programs twice a year, in the fall and in the spring. I like to avoid the winter months as the weather can be bad in Connecticut, and people are often too busy because of the holiday season.

Begin parent orientation by showing the film *Everybody Rides the Carousel*, which is based on Erik Erikson's stages of life. Show footage of the first two stages, "trust vs mistrust" and "autonomy vs self-doubt." Psychoanalyst Erik H. Erikson, who was a disciple of Freud, uses the carousel and its rides to serve as metaphors for life and its stages in his theory of personality development. In stage one the infant learns hope and faith from affection (trust) or a sense of abandonment (mistrust). Stage II deals with autonomy and doubt, in which toddlers try things on their own, make mistakes, and so experience both independence and shame and doubt. The stages in this animated film are illustrated by familiar experiences that convey its message in an easily comprehensible and fun way, and lead to some interesting questions and discussions.

At the orientation it is wise to discourage the bringing of older siblings to subsequent infant sessions, but do not rule this out completely. This should be true of all programs which involve parents. You can point out that both parent and infant receive greater satisfaction if the parent is on a one-on-one basis with the child for whom the program is intended and to whose needs it is geared. Naturally, however, older siblings must come if parents have no alternative, and they will often enjoy this "back to babyhood" time, or they may be content to look at books more appropriate to their "big-boy" or "big-girl" level with the parent near by. Far better they should be at the library than left home, possibly alone.

Siblings who either resent a new brother or sister, or who would like to have books of their own about the new baby, can be given "new baby books"—a list of which appears in Appendix 1 at the back of this book. These books are designed to draw an older child into the "baby experience," and reward the positive feelings toward the infant that the child has.

The actual infant program lasts 60 minutes and follows this loose formula:

1. Talk about a couple of parent books for about 5 minutes.

2. Pass out multiple copies of infant books to the parents. Then read the books or booktalk them. If there are more than one in a series, read one and show the rest. This

should take about 15 minutes, and your books should include board books, vinyl books, cloth books, paperback and hardcover books, foldout books, and peek-a-boo books.

Multiple books become a problem if you have too large an enrollment. However, you can hand out books in a series and do a couple of them. I am talking about books that take no more than 30 seconds to do, such as Helen Oxenbury's five baby board books.

3. Introduce music to the group for 10–15 minutes. Records are the most convenient form of recording to use, as you can find a song more easily on a record than on a cassette or compact disc. However, have cassettes and compact discs available to check out, as parents now seem to prefer them. For the most part the records I use in programs are activity records but it is most effective if you can sing and play a musical instrument or have a parent perform. The parents and children do fingerplays, clap, jump, etc. right along with me even in the infant program. For example, I use songs such as the "Baby's Hokey Pokey" from the *Baby Face* record: the baby lies on her back and the parent or caregiver holds the baby's wrists and gently lifts her arms up and down with the spoken directions. The parent also moves the baby's arms in circles. With "Tickle, Wiggle and Giggle" from the *Diaper Gym* record the parent lightly tickles or shakes the baby playfully. The whole pattern is repeated holding the baby's ankles.

In the infant program I play nursery rhymes and lullabies, sometimes handing out bells or other musical instruments to the parents to go along with the music. For example, a good record to use with bells is Sharon, Lois and Bram's *Mainly Mother Goose*. On that record are two selections, "Ride a Cock Horse" and "Rings on Her Toes." Another example is on the *Baby Record* by Bob McGrath. He has a section on instrument play which includes bell songs, "1, 2, 3, 4 Jingle at the Cottage Door" and "Bell Horses."

There are always some parents who will participate in the clapping, singing, shaking bells, etc., but others are very inhibited and it may take a couple of sessions for them to get into the spirit of the program. The more parents you can involve from the very beginning of the program, the more likelihood of its success. All babies love music so this is an important part of the program.

4. Follow music with toys. Demonstrate how they work for about 10 or 15 minutes. You can do this in more depth with babies than with toddlers or older children because babies will not grab the toys until you put them down.

5. The final part of the program is the interaction of the parents and infants with other parents and infants.

We have built up an extensive toy collection that circulates but you might want to start with an in-house collection. A list of toys for programming with young children is included in chapter 6. Another idea is to have parents or volunteers make toys out of materials found around the house. Some suggestions are:

1. Blocks made out of milk cartons and covered with self-adhesive paper.

2. Boxes, all shapes and sizes. Children love to crawl into big boxes.

3. Shaker bottles. Put dry cereal into clear plastic bottles. If the bottle is opened accidentally, the cereal won't hurt the child—but watch they don't try to swallow it.

4. Hand puppets, made from socks or felt.

5. Containers—plastic containers of all shapes that can be used for putting objects in and dumping them out.

SAMPLE PROGRAMS

The following four sample programs have been used in the Farmington, Connecticut library with a good deal of success. You can borrow these programs or use them as models for programs of your own. Perhaps trying two or three out will give you a better idea of how your library parents respond to them, and you might then want to tailor your programs to more local experiences, i.e., instead of animal sounds you might try the city sounds of subways, trucks, and the like.

Remember, your short term objective is to make parents and infants feel comfortable while pointing out the many activities that they can experience together at home. Parenting is a skill that some mothers and fathers adjust to very easily but many parents need help. Try not to cover too much material in one session. Parents are naturally distracted by their babies and cannot absorb as much information when their babies are present.

Parent and Infant—First Program

I.   Parent books

1. *Babies Need Books* by Dorothy Butler. From her introduction, Butler states, "I believe books should play a prominent part in children's lives from babyhood: that access to books, through parents and other adults, greatly increases a child's chances of becoming a happy and involved human being" (p. vii). She discusses the choice of books from birth to six years of age.

   For the mothers of infants I point out the chapter called "Too Little to Look?" This chapter is especially helpful to parents who are skeptical about reading to a baby. I also explain that because Butler is a New Zealander, our library will not have all the books she is describing.

2. *Reading and Loving* by Leila Berg. All children's first experience of reading should be a loving and sensuous one, so that they can come to discover the power of books for themselves. This is an important book for all parents who wish their children to learn to read with pleasure.

II. Infant Books

1. *Dressing* by Helen Oxenbury. Others in the baby board books series are *Family, Friends, Working* and *Playing*. All five books have the same organization, with the object on the left page and the same object on the right page in some close relationship with a baby. All five books are superior and are extremely popular.

2. *Animals on the Farm* by Kenneth Lilly. Others in the baby animal board books series are *Animals in the Country, Animals of the Ocean, Animals in the Jungle,* and *Animals at the Zoo*. All five books have beautiful, clear life-like drawings of an animal and its young. Start with the book on farm animals.

3. *Teddy Bear Plays in the Water* by Helmut Spanner. A wordless fold-out board book. Others in the series are *Mouse Visits the Kitchen, Bathtime for Mouse,* and *Teddy Bear's Day*. It is fun for the baby to watch the antics of the bear in the water. Suggest to parents that they can place the book on a bureau near the baby's crib at eye level so he can see the colorful illustrations while lying in his crib.

4. *I'm a Baby* by Phoebe Dunn. Babies love looking at photographs of other babies. Here are moments in the daily lives of all babies as they grow and develop. Most babies can really relate to these kinds of books and some parents want to check out only this type of book.

III. Records

1. *The Baby Record* by Bob McGrath. Select these bouncing rhymes, and use a doll to help demonstrate how to do

them: "Ride Baby Ride"; "Mother and Father and Uncle John"; "To Market to Market"; "This Is the Way the Ladies Ride"; "Baby a Go-Go."

Side 1: All finger and toe plays: "This Little Pig Goes to Market"; "Round and Round the Garden"; "These Are Baby's Fingers"; "Slowly, Slowly"; "Let's Go to the Woods"; "Come a Look a See."

Songs: "Head and Shoulders." This is touching different parts of the body. "As I Was Walking to Town One Day." This song describes the different animals you meet and the sounds they make. The record has you meet a dog, a cat, a cow, and a duck but you can insert any animal. It is good to have pictures of the animals that you are meeting.

Lullabies: "Baa Baa Black Sheep"; "Star Light Star Bright."

IV. Toys

Hand out the *List of Selected Toys for Children Under Three* (see chapter 6). Make sure that the toys on your list can circulate. If at all possible try to have multiples of each one.

1. Active Baby (Ambi). From about six months to two years. Four separate simple and beautiful toys. Encourages development of focal skills, eye-hand coordination, and motor skills.

2. Baby's First Car (Ambi). From about six months to three years. Encourages physical activity and coordination and imagination. The child will make the car go forward and backward.

3. Busy Clutch Ball (Child Guidance). From four months to two years. The ball is easy to hold, doesn't roll very far, and is ideal for the child who is crawling. Develops motor coordination.

4. Click-A-Wheel (Kiddicraft). From about six months to three years. This toy produces seven different sounds. It encourages discrimination of sound.

5. Cloth Blocks (Galt). From four months to two years. Baby's first blocks. Six big squeezable blocks to be stacked and knocked down.

V. Interactions with parents, toys, books and babies. This is an important part of the program as many parents need this interaction. Make sure there are enough toys so that every infant has a chance to handle them.

Parent and Infant—Second Program

I. Parent books

1. *The First Relationship: Mother and Infant* by Daniel Stern. This book focuses on the details of the way mother and infant behave together as they go through their daily routine.
2. *The First Three Years of Life* by Burton L. White. In this informative guide for parents, Dr. White divides the first thirty-six months of life into seven stages of growth and gives a comprehensive list of do's and don't's. His book covers all areas of child development and such topics as toys, equipment, crying, and creative discipline.

II. Infant books

1. *The Great Big Book of Nursery Rhymes* by Peggy Blakely. This is a wonderful nursery rhyme book for the very young child. The verse is on the left and the very colorful illustration is on the right so the child can easily associate the illustration with the rhyme.
2. *The Real Mother Goose Husky Book I* by Blanche Fisher Wright. There are four husky books which have eighteen verses in each one from the original edition published in 1916. They are easy-to-hold board books and each verse has its own illustration.

3. *A First Book: In My Kitchen* by Brimax (Object Lesson series). Also *In My Nursery* and *In My Garden*. Highly stylized illustrations outlined in black with excellent figure-ground contrast against solid color backgrounds.

4. *Animal Sounds* by Aurelius Battaglia. Infants love to hear animal sounds! The illustrations are delightful and clear and the book encourages parents and infants to have wonderful sound activities together. This is a book I encourage every parent to buy and use over and over again with their child.

III. Records

1. *Nursery Rhymes* by Ella Jenkins. "The Muffin Man"; "Hey Diddle Diddle"; "Humpty Dumpty"; "Little Miss Muffet." Most babies especially like "The Muffin Man."

2. *Creative Play Songs, Volume I* by Stepping Tones. "Incy Wincy Spider"; "Open Them Shut Them."

IV. Toys

1. Baby's First Fone (Ambi). From about six months to three years. Encourages discrimination of sound and the development of manual dexterity, modeling behavior, and imagination.

2. Threading Shapes, Set I (Brio). From about ten months to two years. Both the balls and cubes are a pleasure to rattle, mouthe, and teethe on. First with the balls, later with the cubes, they are a challenge to thread through the plastic disks.

3. Crawl-A-Ball (Discovery). From about four months to eighteen months. This is a ball to grab, gum, and chew on. It rolls only a few feet and barely bounces. Encourages development of focal attention.

4. Handy Boxes (Ambi). From about six months to beyond three years. There are six nesting boxes with bottoms and tops. The infant will only investigate the bottoms.

5. Rock 'n Roll (Ambi). From one month to eighteen months. The rattle, rolling, and balancing provide immediate and varied responses to the child's initiating action. This encourages motor activity.

V. Interaction with the parents, toys, books, and babies. Use animal puppets to reinforce the book *Animal Sounds*.

🐾 Parent and Infant—Third Program

I. Parent books

1. *This Little Puffin: Finger Plays and Nursery Games* by Elizabeth Matterson. This is a remarkable treasury of fingerplays and singing and action games to use with very young children, either in groups or individually.

2. *Your Baby Needs Music* by Barbara Cass-Beggs. The author wrote this book to help parents use music to aid their baby's development.

II. Infant books

1. *Reading* by Jan Omerod. (Also *Dad's Back*, *Messy Baby*, and *Sleeping*). These books are about fathers and babies together and show a delightful family life.

2. *All Fall Down* by Helen Oxenbury. (Also *Tickle, Tickle*, *Clap Hands* and *Say Goodnight*). Rollicking, tumbling babies moving and jumping and falling around. A vibrant and alive series, done in board.

3. *At My House* by Margaret Miller. (Also *In My Room*, *Me and My Clothes*, and *Time to Eat*). Children learn to talk by naming the familiar things they see around them. These four board books help them.

4. *Sweet Dreams, Spot* by Eric Hill. (Also *Spot's Toys*, *Spot's Friends*, and *Spot Goes Splash*). These foam-filled vinyl books can be used in the bath tub.

III. Records

1. *Finger Plays and Foot Plays* by Rosemary Hallum and Henry Glass. "I Have Ten Little Fingers"; "Five Little Monkeys"; "The Wheels on the Bus."
2. *Songs to Grow On* by Woody Guthrie. "Put Your Finger in the Air"; "Cleano."

IV. Toys

1. Baby Toy Set (Ambi). From three months to eighteen months. This set includes a Rota Rattle with a suction cup on the bottom, a baby bell which rolls, and a Handy Dandy Rattle.
2. Flip Fingers (Kiddicraft). From six months to two years. Encourages exploration and "flipping" by baby. A very simple toy which gives a lot of satisfaction.
3. Telephone Rattle (Kiddicraft). From three to twelve months. A colorful rattle with a dial that rotates and clicks. Good gripping and biting surface.
4. Turn and Learn Activity Center (Fisher Price). From six months to thirty months. This four-sided floor toy has a spinning base with a different activity on each side, and a mirror on one side for peek-a-boo play.
5. Barrel Jack (Ambi). From ten months to two years. Clown makes funny movements when it is rolled on a smooth floor.

V. Interaction with parents, toys, books, and babies.

✿ Parent and Infant—Fourth Program

I.   Parent books

1. *Toys and Playthings* by John and Elizabeth Newson. A common sense approach to play in a full and practical

discussion of toys and the developing child, with down-to-earth suggestions for parents and professionals.

2. *How to Play with Your Child* by Brian and Shirley Sutton-Smith. Beginning at the time of birth and on up to age thirteen, the Sutton-Smiths demonstrate what children are likely to be doing at every different level and suggest ways parents can stimulate play at these stages.

II. Infant books

1. *In the Morning* by Anne Rockwell. (Also in this board book series are *At Night, At the Playground,* and *In the Rain.* Bright clear illustrations and a simple text highlight familiar objects and activities in a young child's world.

2. *Catch Me and Kiss Me and Say It Again,* by Clyde Watson. A rollicking collection of rhymes. Choose three or four of them to do with the group.

3. *Round and Round the Garden* by Sarah Williams. A delightful collection of play rhymes. There is an illustration at the bottom of each page showing how to do the fingerplays that go with the rhymes.

4. *Who?* by Leo Lionni. (Others in the series are *When?, Where?,* and *What?*). This wordless board book poses questions, but right answers are not important. The purpose of these books is to engage the eye and mind of the young child.

III. Records

1. *Baby Face* by Georgiana Stewart. "Baby Face"; "Yes, Sir, That's My Baby"; "Baby's Hokey Pokey"; "It's Small World."

2. *Diaper Gym* by Priscilla Hegner. "Cuddle Up a Little Closer"; "Bow 'n' Arrow"; "Puss 'n' Boots"; "Pat Your

Little Feet"; "Pat Your Little Hands"; "Baby Hop"; "My Little Hands."

IV. Toys

1. Skwish (Pappa Geppetto's Toys). From three months to all ages. The design of this fascinating, multidimensional toy makes it especially easy for babies to grasp and manipulate. They are intrigued by the sight and sound of sliding bears and bells and, of course, the "skwish."

2. Double Feature Baby Mirror and Visual Display (Wimmer-Ferguson). A sparkling, clear baby mirror with an eye-catching "seascape" of black and white graphics for infants from birth on up. Babies love mirrors and eagerly respond to their own faces. From birth to three months, babies are more attracted to high-contrast patterns than to color or brightness.

3. Play Train (Kiddicraft). From six to eighteen months. One of the first push-alongs which encourages finger manipulation and two-handed coordination.

4. Wobble Globe (Kiddicraft). From six months. The colored balls rattle noisily as they are flicked on the flexible rubber stem which attaches to a surface by a suction cup.

5. Magic Man (Ambi). This magic man remains astride the ball as it rolls across the floor. A really fun toy.

EVALUATION

It is very important to do an evaluation of all programs. With diminishing library budgets, the children's staff should document the need for their services. Library boards and town boards like to have this documentation in writing. In programs where there is parent-child participation, I ask the parents to fill out a very simple evaluation form. The form has to be short (or they won't fill it out) and you need their input.

These are the evaluation questions I use with the infant, toddler, and two-year-old programs:

1. Do you think this program is worthwhile? If yes, why? If no, why?
2. What do you like best about this program?
3. What do you like least about the program?
4. How would you change it?

These are general responses you are likely to hear from your evaluation:

1. Find it very helpful to meet other mothers and babies.
2. Learn about all the materials that the library has for infants.
3. Really enjoy the toys and music.
4. Would like the program to run longer than an hour and with more than six sessions.

It is unlikely you will hear much criticism of your program but if you do, think it over honestly and see if you should re-work parts of what you are doing. Remember that caregivers are your allies and give-and-take with them will only improve your program and justify it when budget time comes.

3

Programs for Toddler I and Toddler II

The toddler program is a continuation of the infant program, and it too is aimed largely at the caregiver. This time, however, the child is much more active physically and so the sessions need to move briskly along. The toddler attention span is short—a few minutes at most—and they respond to drama. So here is an opportunity for ham actors and actresses to read aloud with gusto!

Begin your toddler program by scheduling ten to twelve sessions of about 45 minutes apiece, and have two toddler groups. I now register fifteen children for each group, but if this is your first time, limit it to eight or ten children. You can increase the number when you become more experienced in doing the program. The first group could be Toddler I, children ages one year to twenty-four months; and the second group could be Toddler II, children from twenty to twenty-four months old. At the end of the toddler spectrum you might include those children who had "graduated" from your infant program. They would have had the benefit of programs in the library, and would likely respond more quickly to what you were doing. Their parents would too. Otherwise, you need to divide the children as best you can along developmental lines so that each one is comfortable with the group level.

This may not be easy to do at first, but after a few sessions you might see children who would be better placed in the other toddler group, and could suggest this to the parent. Of course other age divisions are possible too, but in large part this depends on the preferences of your library staff and the number of children in the program.

One of the greatest roadblocks to smooth functioning of the toddler program is not really the restless, active toddler, but the parent. In these programs as in the infant program you must underscore to parents the importance of the one-on-one relationship with their child. In her book, *Booksharing: 101 Programs to Use with Preschoolers*, librarian Margaret Read MacDonald points out:

> It is important that the children stay on their parents' lap or cuddle near them. This keeps the parent-child functioning as an interested unit and participating in storytime as a whole. If the children move away from the parents, both parent and child begin to interact with peers and soon no one is paying attention to the storytime activity. Parents are worse offenders at this than are the children. (p. 4)

It is crucial to stress this in the toddler program and to keep talking about it right along. It takes only one parent not reacting with their own child to disrupt everything you are trying to do.

STRUCTURE OF THE TODDLER PROGRAM

Everyone sits on the floor in a semicircle, or in chairs with the child on the parent's lap. Greet each child as they come in, make small talk with caregivers, and take attendance. Unlike the infant program, you will not begin with parent books. These books should be displayed and book lists available to give out. Many parents will have questions about them, but you can defer those until the end of the session. At this point, you need to get off to a brisk start to keep the toddlers' attention from wandering. You can plunge right in with books.

You should usually include a peek-a-boo book or flap book, an interaction book, and a rhyming book in each session. Toddlers do not necessarily need a storyline, but they enjoy looking at number and alphabet books which they view purely as object books. Wordless books always have to be introduced to parents, for otherwise they don't see the value of them until they are used in the group. The whole storyline must be clear from the illustrations alone, which means parent or child can tell the story in their own words. You can add zest to the readings by a little amateur dramatics on your own part. Handling of board books, too, is to be encouraged with toddlers. They see these as real books, but are apt to be hard on them. Some bar codes get chewed off but fortunately board books are nearly indestructible, and with the goal of making books a part of a child's life, a little gnawing is a minor problem in the scheme of things. We call board books "bread and butter" books for the toddler, and encourage parents to have a shelf of them for the child to reach and use at home. At the same time, we suggest that parents use "regular" books with the child and explore these books together—but keep them safely out of reach until the child understands how to care for them.

All the books in the sample toddler programs to follow are high interest. We follow the criteria of what children like and what their interests are in our selections. Toddlers are fascinated by other children their own age or younger and all kinds of animals. They are interested in their own bodies and love to do fingerplays that describe their body parts. The toddlers have to be able to identify with what goes on in the book. In other words, the experience in the book must already be in their background. Usually three or four books are listed for each program but in the beginning you may want to read only one or two. It depends upon your group. When the children are accustomed to the routine, and know that playtime is coming at the end, they are more ready to settle down and read books at the beginning.

Following the books, put on a couple of action records so the toddlers can move around. The more the parents participate, the more the children will—although not necessarily the first few times. It is a slow process to get some children to react to you, because for many it is the first time they are interacting with an adult they don't already know. By playing two records, you can expose caregivers to the many good recordings the library has and which they could also use at home.

In Toddler I, however, many of the children cannot yet walk, let alone dance. Here is where fingerplays fit in, and if you have not yet discovered their tremendous power and versatility, you will now. Fingerplays are a vital part of early childhood programs. They can be defined as little action verses and songs involving movement of fingers. Not only do the children have a lot of fun doing fingerplays, they are a great learning experience. Many things happen with fingerplays, such as:

- Using small muscles of the body
- Learning body parts by names
- Experiencing the fun of rhythm
- Advancing vocabularies
- Participating in the joys of repetition
- Relaxing and performing motions with music
- Sharpening concentration

Most of the fingerplays in the sample programs are set to music.

With this action break over, it is time to hand out Arrowroot cookies and settle the parents and children down for a film. In the Toddler I group you will find that the film is marginal as far as the children are concerned, but it is good to expose the parents early so they can learn to evaluate good visual experiences for their children. There is a great deal of passive TV exposure with some year-old children and it is essential to try to educate parents away from this sort of nonactivity. Showing films answers both parents' need for visual entertainment and your concealed purpose of exposing adults to as much good material for children as you can. The recommended films here also have, in many instances, recommended activities to accompany them. In any case, the films must be animated and have a catchy, bouncy, musical score—and they must be short. By Toddler II, the children really respond much more to the films—often because they are by that time familiar with them—and most children will watch for three or four minutes.

Round off the toddler program with toys. You need to provide plenty of them to avoid conflict among eager children. You can demonstrate to parents how the toys work, and build activities around the musical instruments, puppets, blocks, boxes and other toys recommended here as appropriate to this age.

MATERIALS FOR LIBRARIES WITH LIMITED RESOURCES

Not all libraries are fortunate enough to enjoy the funding that will buy everything in the programs to follow. Others may not want to invest until they have seen results of a pilot program, or may want to phase in materials year by year. This should not deter determined children's librarians, many of whom already are practiced scavengers who can make do under less-than-perfect circumstances. Remember that the programs presented here can be used on a smaller scale if need be, with a little imagination and thought thrown in on your part.

Here are suggestions for starting toddler and two-year-old programs when your resources are limited. For around $1,000 you could outfit your library with multiple copies of thirty-one children's books, a set of cardboard blocks, a set of musical instruments (fifteen pieces), animal puppets, and four records or cassettes. This can get you going.

The books used here are either paperback or board books, with some exceptions. This collection should be kept in house solely for the programming purposes, and not allowed to circulate. This way the books can be used over and over again for different story hour sessions. Duplicates of these books and similar books should be displayed so that they can be checked out to use at home. Several smaller or branch libraries might cooperate and finance the project by applying for a grant or asking community groups for help, and then rotating the collection. Five or six story hours for each age group could then be scheduled for groups of eight children and their caregivers.

Substantial savings can be realized by photocopying fingerplays and using them extensively. Spend time in your sessions teaching parents the fingerplays; they can carry the program spirit into the home through fingerplays and stories. By telling stories as well as reading books to the children, you are meeting interaction and language needs. Such perennial favorites as "Goldilocks and the Three Bears," "The Three Little Pigs," "The Billy Goats Gruff," and others are easily remembered by parents and caregivers, and afford much pleasure to adult and child alike in the telling.

Music is an essential ingredient of the toddler and two-year-old programs and must be included, so I have selected records that have a wide variety of songs to appeal to the children, many of them activity songs. Singing together should be encouraged—many parents will pick up lyrics easily and can be encouraged to sing to their child in the car, when they do housework, before bedtime, and so forth. Since small children will not be able to remember a full song, explain to parents how they can include a "special" part in a song for children—for instance, in "Pufferbellies" the child could chime in on the "Puff puff, Toot toot" part. The important thing is that it be done together and it be fun for both.

Of all the toys the most basic to the needs of this age group are blocks, puppets, and musical instruments. The range of these materials is a wide one, and they can be enjoyed by the developmentally youngest child as well as the oldest. Chapter 6 explains the cognitive processes developed by using such toys. Of course, toy drives and donations can expand your toy collection quickly, but good basic sets of these classic toys are an absolute necessity for the library in any case.

What must be left out of the programs are films. Unless your library already has ones that you can commandeer, or that you can get on inter-library loan or video store rental, the cost per film is high for a single library on a limited budget. As the toddlers and two-year-olds are an active bunch, they will not miss the films if kept busy with toys and fingerplays. You will, unfortunately, lose valuable tools for educating parents toward good film and away from daytime TV.

The cost projected for a limited resources program are based on 1992 prices with the books figured at a 40% discount off list price. Eight copies of each book are included.

⚞ Books: Toddler group

All Gone by Sarah Garland
Animal Sounds by Aurelius Battaglia
Dear Zoo by Rod Campbell
Ding Dong! and Other Sounds by Christina Salac Dubov
Freight Train by Donald Crews
Goodnight Moon (paper and board) by Margaret Wise Brown
I Can Build a House by Shigeo Watanabe
Oh, No! by Sarah Garland
1, 2, 3 to the Zoo by Eric Carle
Our Day by Lucy Dickens
Pat-A-Cake by Moira Kemp
Round and Round the Garden by Moira Kemp
Toot, Toot by Brian Wildsmith
When We Went to the Park by Shirley Hughes
Where's the Baby? by Cheryl Christian

⚞ Books: Two-year-old group

Birthday Card, Where Are You? by Harriet Ziefert
The Carrot Seed by Ruth Krauss
Good Morning, Chick by Mirra Ginsburg
How Do I Put It On? by Shigeo Watanabe

Noisy by Shirley Hughes
Peek-A-Boo! by Janet and Alan Ahlberg
Roll Over by Mordicai Gerstein
Rosie's Walk by Pat Hutchins
Sam Who Never Forgets by Eve Rice
Sam's Wagon by Barbro Lindgren
Sheep in a Jeep by Nancy Shaw
Ten, Nine, Eight by Molly Bang
Truck by Donald Crews
What's for Lunch? by Eric Carle
Who Sank the Boat? by Pamela Allen
Whose Mouse Are You? by Robert Kraus

🎵 Records or Cassettes

Fun Activities for Toddlers by Laura Johnson
Songs to Grow On by Woody Guthrie
If You're Happy and You Know It Sing Along with Bob, Volume II
   by Bob McGrath
Finger Plays and Foot Plays by Rosemary Hallum

🎵 Budget

$312.00	Toddler books
400.00	Two-year-old books
44.00	Records
39.95	Set of cardboard blocks (48)
36.95	Rhythm Band Set: primary set of fifteen instruments
74.95	Animal puppets, set of twelve. (Childcraft Class Menagerie) or other puppets
$907.85	Total

SAMPLE PROGRAMS

🐾 Toddler I - First Program

I. Multiple copies of toddler books to read aloud

1. *Animal Sounds* by Aurelius Battaglia. Use with puppets and make the sounds of the farm animals. Toddlers love to do this!

2. *The Very Busy Spider* by Eric Carle. In this multi-sensory book the children can feel the pictures as well as see them. They have the tactile experience of feeling the spider's web as it grows from a single thread to a complex creation. Again, make the sounds of the farm animals.

3. *Where's Spot?* by Eric Hill. A peek-a-boo book with great parent and child interaction in potential acting out of the story. This can be used with a little stuffed dog Spot.

II. Records and fingerplays

1. *One Light, One Sun* by Raffi. Play the song "Down on Grandpa's Farm." On Grandpa's farm there is a big brown cow, a little red hen, a little white sheep, a big black dog and a big brown horse. The children like to make all the animal sounds.

2. *Finger Plays and Foot Plays* by Rosemary Hallum and Henry Glass. "Five Little Monkeys," "The Wheels on the Bus," "I Have Ten Little Fingers," are three of the fingerplays on this record. There are nine more, some of which are footplays. Prepare the lyrics as a hand-out so parents can sing along with you and later do it again at home.

3. Fingerplays

   • "Trot trot to Boston
   Trot trot to Lynn

Trot trot to Boston
And then trot back again!"

Show caregivers how to bounce their babies gently on their foot or knees to give a horse ride.

- "Round around the garden
  Like a teddy bear
  One step, two steps
  Tickle you under there."

  Show caregivers how to draw circles on their baby's palms and then walk their fingers up baby's arm "creepy mouse" style and then tickle the baby gently.

III. Film: *Rosie's Walk* (5 minutes) based on *Rosie's Walk* by Pat Hutchins. Rosie the hen goes for a walk around the farm yard. Right behind her is the fox who is trying to catch up to her. Rosie has a very uneventful walk but the fox gets into all kinds of difficulties. The animation is delightful, but it is the American folk tune, "Turkey in the Straw," that captivates children. Walk and strut around the room with your group.

IV. Toys: Farm animal puppets and farm animal play figures, Fisher Price farm and farmyard animals, animal sound containers. The last toy makes the sound of the farm come to life when you turn each container over. You hear a cow, a kitten, a lamb or a bird. You need a nice variety of large farm animal puppets. Both the children and the adults enjoy making the sounds for the puppets. This is one activity that the parents enter into without much leadership, as do the children.

🐾 Toddler I—Second Program

I.   Multiple copies of toddler books to read aloud

1. *How Do I Put It On?* by Shiego Watanabe. Act out this book—put a hat on your feet, put shoes on your head. There is great humor in the role reversal—children will

be fascinated by the fact that you don't seem to be very bright. Their self-confidence is really boosted by knowing more than you seem to. This is a device that parents can use quite often at home to bolster their child's sense of capability.

2. *Sam's Lamp* by Barbro Lindgren. This book is one of a series about a toddler named Sam. All toddlers really relate to Sam because, like them, he blames other things and people for what happens, though he initiates the action and it is clearly his fault. In this case, Sam climbs up to see the lamp and he falls. He naturally blames the lamp and not himself. This is a perfectly normal reaction in a toddler, and this book provides an explanation to parents who have wondered about this behavior. Another good example of this theme to use with a slightly older child is the Mercer Mayer book, *Just for You*.

3. *Peek-A-Boo* by Mitsumasa Anno. In this wordless peek-a-boo book, Anno conjures up a surprise on every page. The peek-a-boo hands are in front of a rabbit, a dog, a cat, a lion, a tiger, a mother, a child, a daddy, a pig, a fox, a raccoon, a clown and a Santa Claus.

II.   Fingerplays: Parts of Your Body

- "Clap Your Hands"

  "Clap your hands, clap your hands
  Clap them just like me.
  Touch your shoulders, touch your shoulders
  Touch them just like me.
  Tap your knees, tap your knees
  Tap them just like me.
  Shake your head, shake your head
  Shake it just like me.
  Clap your hands, clap your hands
  Now let them quiet be."

- "Ten Fingers"

  "I have ten little fingers and they all belong to me.
  I can make them do things. Would you like to see?
  I can shut them up tight, or open them wide. I can put
      them together, or make them hide.
  I can make them jump high,
  I can make them jump low.
  I can fold them quietly and hold them just so."

III. Records

1. *Songs to Grow On* by Woody Guthrie. A classic record
   that has sixteen favorite songs on it. Woody Guthrie
   sings slowly which meets the needs of many children.

   - "Put Your Finger in the Air." A fingerplay to music
     that deals with the parts of the body. The child uses
     his finger to touch his cheek, his nose, his head, etc.
   - "Cleano." Children love this one. Have them pretend
     to take a bath with you.
   - "Dance Around." Get up and dance around, fly
     around, march around, etc. If a child cannot walk,
     the parent can do the action with the child in her
     arms.

IV. Film: *Matrioska* (5 minutes). This film about dancing stacking Russian dolls is set to zestful music. There are seven dolls that fit inside each other but spend most of the time dancing and spinning around. You can use it to lead into a discussion of stacking toys and why they are so good for hand-eye coordination.

V. Toys: Stacking Toys

1. Handy Boxes (Ambi). Six boxes of varying colors and
   sizes that can be used as a pile-up or nesting cups.

2. Stack 'n' Store Nesting Cubes (Little Tikes). These five cubes can all be stacked to build a tower 20″ high. Also, cubes can nest inside each other.

3. Rock-A-Stack (Fisher Price). Six rings fit over a cone, which rocks back and forth on a rounded base.

4. Matrioska (Fisher Price). A stacking toy like the toy in the movie discussed previously. You can have a five-doll matrioska, a seven-doll matrioska—up to twenty stacking dolls.

5. Measure Up (Discovery). A set of twelve durable plastic containers, each with an animal shape at the bottom.

6. Roller Coaster (Anatex). A fascinating three-dimensional toy that has colorful beads that move along on looping safety wires in several directions. Improves eye-hand coordination and motor skills.

✋ Toddler I—Third Program

I.   Multiple copies of toddler books to read aloud

1. *Dear Zoo* by Rod Campbell. A peek-a-boo book with zoo animals which also comes in a small edition. The child writes to the zoo for a pet. They send an elephant, a giraffe, a lion, a camel, a monkey, a frog and finally a dog. The dog is perfect so the child keeps him.

2. *1, 2, 3 to the Zoo* by Eric Carle. This book is more sophisticated but it is a great delight. Use it to identify animals more than as a counting book with toddlers. The children point out the different animals and take them to the zoo in a train.

3. *Noisy* by Shirley Hughes. A toddler and her brother listen to all kinds of noises. Although the illustrations are quite busy, the children really relate to this book and others in her nursery collection series, such as

Bathwater's Hot, When We Went to the Park, Two Shoes, New Shoes, Colors, and *All Shapes and Sizes.*

II. Records

1. *More Singable Songs* by Raffi. Song: "Shake My Sillies Out." This song always gets the kids moving and makes them happy. The children shake their sillies out, clap their crazies out, jump their jiggles out, yawn their sleepies out and wiggle their waggles away.

2. *Music for 1's and 2's* by Tom Glazer. Song: "Where Are Your Eyes?" This is another fingerplay set to music. One of the first early childhood records to be issued, it remains a favorite.

III. Fingerplays

- "Two little blackbirds sitting on a hill
  (close fists, extend thumbs)
  One named Jack and the other named Jill
  (talk to each thumb)
  Fly away Jack; fly away Jill
  (toss thumbs over shoulders separately)
  Come back Jack; come back Jill."
  (bring back fists separately with thumbs extended)

- "This little pig went to market
  (point to each finger in turn)
  This little pig stayed home.
  This little pig had roast beef,
  This little pig had none.
  This little pig cried wee, wee, wee,
  (run hands behind back)
  All the way home."

IV. Film: *Chicken Soup with Rice.* A film that really makes you want to dance and sing. It is from the animated film *Really Rosie* starring the Nutshell Kids. The movie was adapted from the

Nutshell Library by Maurice Sendak and *The Sign on Rosie's Door* by Maurice Sendak. The *Nutshell Library* consists of four books: *Chicken Soup with Rice*; *One Was Johnny*; *Pierre*; and *Alligators All Around*. The films from the *Nutshell Library* can be purchased separately and they run from two minutes to six minutes. *Really Rosie* is 30 minutes long. The music by Carole King and the animation are super.

V. Activity-Record: *Singable Songs for the Very Young* by Raffi. Song, "Going to the Zoo." This song has a wonderful rhythm and is great to use with musical instruments. Play it a couple of times and have the children experiment with more than one musical instrument. The instruments that you use should be rhythm instruments such as cymbals, tambourines, maracas, sandblocks, wrist bells, bells on handles, and sleigh bells.

VI. Toys

1. Zoo Animals (Willis). This set of five vinyl zoo animals includes a giraffe, an elephant, a lion, a zebra, and a polar bear.
2. Zoo Animals (Fisher Price). There are six colorful and playful wooden animals printed on both sides.
3. Zoo animal puppets (Dakin). A hippo, an elephant, a monkey, a kangaroo, a lion, an ostrich, a bear, and a snake are possibilities, but whatever exotic animals you come up with will do. The children like the animal puppets best as you can make them seem to come alive and talk to the children. At this age it is better to use the hand puppets that can fit on your hand or the child's hand.

Toddler I—Fourth Program

I. Multiple copies of toddler books to read aloud

1. *Oh, No!* by Sarah Garland. A toddler goes to visit Grandma and gets into lots of trouble. One mischief activity right after another. Absolutely delightful.

2. *The Toy Box* by Mary H. Heyward. A lift-the-flap book in which toddlers have a great time finding the toys and putting them away in the toy box.

3. *Are You My Mother?* and *Are You My Daddy?* by Carla Dijs. Two pop-up books. The first one has a little chick looking for mother and the second one has a little tiger looking for daddy.

4. *Touch! Touch!* by Riki Levinson. The toddler in this book touches everything in sight with hilarious results. He touches the cat on the counter who spills a bowl of cake mix which the dog walks through and then puts his paws on the sister and so it goes. Parents can really appreciate this book as they know how much trouble their own toddler can make as he goes about exploring his world.

II. Records

1. *Early Early Childhood Songs* by Ella Jenkins. Song: "Mary Had a Little Lamb."

2. *Raindrops* by Sharron Lucky. Song: "Where is Thumbkin?"

III. Film: *Hush Little Baby* (5 minutes). This is an enchanting rendition of the traditional folk lullaby. Parents can cuddle their babies and sing along as the words are flashed on the screen.

IV. Musical Toys

1. Merry Go Round (Battat). A top, which requires minimal pressure to push down to make butterflies dance around. The butterflies are enclosed under plastic and as they go around, a bell rings.

2. Piano (Battat). This is a four-note piano that has a bear on top which spins as the music plays.

3. Rolling Bells (Battat). Rich-sounding bells in a little four-wheeled vehicle.

4. Accordion (Battat). As the child plays the accordion, brightly colored balls whirl around in the see-through compartment.

5. Xylo Drum (Fisher Price). Two musical instruments in one: a xylophone on one side and a drum on the other.

6. Chime Ball (Fisher Price). A chime rings out and figures move in this roly-poly ball.

7. Melody Push Chime (Fisher Price). A child pushes this musical roller chime designed with storybook figures. As the roller chime goes around, it makes music.

Toddler II - First Program

I. Multiple copies of toddler books to read aloud

1. *Roll Over* by Mordicai Gerstein. Real rhythm book with fold-out flaps. There were ten in the bed when the little one said, "Roll over," and the toddler keeps going until there is nobody left. A great bedtime book.

2. *Hand, Hand, Finger, Thumb* by Al Perkins. An *I Can Read* book that toddlers love because of the rhythm. It can be read in programs all the way up to the six-year-old level. The rhythm is contagious and the monkeys are glorious.

3. *Oh Dear!* by Rod Campbell. This is a pull-out flap book with farm animals and sounds. Buster tries to find some eggs and asks several animals before he finally finds the eggs in the hen house.

4. *Old Mother Hubbard* by Colin and Jacqui Hawkins. Flap book of an old favorite nursery rhyme.

5. *Baby in the Box* by Frank Asch. Blocks in the box, baby in the box, and fox and ox in the box. A great book to act out at the end of story hour when the children are playing with blocks and cardboard boxes.

II. Records

1. *Songs About Me* by William Janiak. Song: "Piece of Paper." Each child is given a piece of scrap paper and all have to do different things with it, including blowing the paper, stamping on the paper, shaking the paper, etc., until they crumple it up and throw it in the basket.

2. *It's Toddler Time* by Carol Hammett. Songs: "The Hokey Pokey," "Head, Shoulder, Knees, and Toes," "If You're Happy and You Know It." The hokey pokey is always fun to do with young children. They like to put different parts of their body into the circle, shake them out, and then turn completely around.

III. Film: *Changes, Changes* (6 minutes). Based on the rather sophisticated book *Changes, Changes* by Pat Hutchins, this film has strong, rhythmic, jolly music. Two wooden dolls rearrange a set of wooden blocks to resolve the problems they face. For instance, they make a house in the beginning but it catches on fire, so they make a fire engine out of the blocks to put out the fire. There is so much water around from putting out the fire they make a boat and so on through the movie. The film helps parents see the possibilities and value of blocks.

IV. Toys: Block Play. All of the blocks, with the exception of Baby's First Blocks, are from Childcraft. Give parents a handout from *The Block Book* by Elizabeth Hirsch. There is a chart of potential contributions of blocks for early childhood curriculum. This includes physical development, mathematics, social studies, social development, science, art, and language arts.

1. Bristle Blocks. Soft bristle blocks push together in almost any position, rewarding even the least skillful builder.

2. Magnet Blocks. Easy to put together and easy to pull apart.

3. Bucket of Wood Blocks. A huge set of 100 wood blocks.

4. Unit Wooden Blocks. Selected hardrock northern maple beveled on all edges.

5. Multicolored Building Blocks made of corrugated fiber-board so they are light in weight but super strong. These are the easiest for toddlers to use.

6. Baby's First Blocks (Hand-in-Hand). In this real construction set made of hardwood, blocks lock into place to make building easier.

7. Cardboard boxes. You can get these anywhere but the ones that books come in are a good size (about 19½" x 13" x 9"). Make sure each child has one and can act out *Baby in a Box* by Frank Asch.

⚘ Toddler II - Second Program

I.   Multiple copies of toddler books to read aloud

1. *Jesse Bear, What Will You Wear?* by Nancy White Carlstrom. Lots of rhythm as Jesse Bear goes through the day. Includes one of the nicest illustrations of a father coming home from work that there is in children's literature.

2. *William, Where Are You?* by Mordicai Gerstein. A fold-out flap book that makes looking for William lots of fun.

3. *Freight Train* by Donald Crews. The movement is delightful as the freight train goes across the pages.

4. *Big Wheels* by Anne Rockwell. Many children love this book because the interest in trucks and other large vehicles is so great. This book deals with bulldozers, cranes, dump trucks, cement mixers, and other big wheels.

II. Records

1. *Creative Play Songs: Volume 1* by Stepping Tones. Song: "Wheels on the Bus." An old favorite that parents may know.

"The wheels on the bus go round and round
Round and round, round and round.
The wheels on the bus go round and round
All through the town."

This is the first and last verse with other verses in between. In the other verses, the people go up and down, the windshield wipers go swish, the ladies go yakkaty-yak, etc.

2. *Activity Songs for Kids* by Marcia Berman. Songs: "Tug Boats," about the boat that pushes and pulls other boats all day, and "Doing Things," which has the children clapping, running, jumping, and sleeping. There are also two lovely lullabies.

III. Film: *Red Ball Express* (4 minutes). An abstract animated film of trains and wheels racing across the screen. Delightful, pulsating music is in the background.

IV. Toys

1. Big Wooden Trains and Trucks (Childcraft). Includes trains, dump trucks, pick-up trucks, bulldozers, jeep, etc.

2. Big Safety Signs and Stop Light (Childcraft). Actually turns red, yellow and green because it is battery-operated.

3. Block Play Traffic Signs (Childcraft). Authentic replicas of international traffic signs which bring safety concepts to dramatic play.

Toddler II—Third Program

I.   Multiple copies of toddler books to read aloud

1. *Spot Goes to the Farm* by Eric Hill. Same format as *Where's Spot?*, which is asking a question and finding the

answer behind a movable flap. Spot visits his dad at work
on the farm and looks for baby animals.

2. *Mr. Brown Can Moo, Can You?* by Dr. Seuss. A book of
sounds for children to imitate. The rhythm is delightful.

3. *Hector Protector* by Maurice Sendak. Great book for
dramatic play. Children can identify with Hector Protector, who didn't like to be dressed in green to go to see
the queen. The illustrations are glorious.

II. Records

1. *Fun Activities for Toddlers* by Laura Johnson. Songs:
"Follow Me" and "You Are My Sunshine." "Follow Me"
is a song where the toddlers do everything you do— from
turning around, touching the ground, identifying different parts of the body, and hugging their moms. With
"You Are My Sunshine" the children pretend to be seeds
that grow up to be trees.

III. Fingerplay: "Incy Wincy Spider." I use my whole hands as
the spider climbing up the waterspout, and my hands with fingers
wiggling to suggest the rain falling down. Otherwise, toddlers
have a hard time trying to oppose thumb and index finger in
creating spider movement.

- "The incy wincy spider climbed up the waterspout.
Down came the rain and washed the spider out.
Out came the sun and dried up all the rain,
(*form a circle over your head with your arms*)
So the incy wincy spider climbed up the spout again."

IV. Film: *Incy Wincy Spider* (5 minutes). Children are presented
with a group of animal characters in three all-time favorite
nursery rhymes: "Incy Wincy Spider"; "Little Miss Muffet"; and
"Humpty Dumpty." The film is animated and the rhymes are
introduced by Quincy the spider who has a problem making

friends at first because he is a spider. Recite "Little Miss Muffet" and "Humpty Dumpty" before you show the film.

V. Toys

1. Very simple puzzles

   • Knobbed Fruit Puzzle (Salco). This "first" puzzle has four familiar fruit pieces with large knobs.
   • First Step Knobbed Puzzles (Salco). Tools, four pieces; Hats, five pieces; first toys, four pieces; transportation, five pieces.

2. Push and pull toys

   • Corn Popper (Fisher Price). As the wheels turn on this bright push toy, colored balls jump around inside a clear cylinder and make a popping noise.
   • Flying Octopus (Kouvalias). This pull toy features colored balls on springs above a caterpillar. It makes a marvelous giddy movement when brought to rest and turns and rattles when pulled. The name, however, is perplexing.
   • The Neat New Toy (Kinderworks). As you push this toy, four wooden cylinders move around all with many colored balls sticking out from their sides. Two of the wooden cylinders go up and down and two wooden cylinders go parallel with the floor. It also makes a clacking noise.

༄ Toddler II - Fourth Program

I.   Multiple copies of toddler books to read aloud

1. *All Gone* by Sarah Garland. Share a day with a baby and play a game of "Now you see it, now you don't." A companion volume to *Oh, No!*

2. *Fat Mouse* by Harry Stevens. A delightful board book about a fat mouse who chases a cook, who chases a farmer, etc., until it comes full circle and the cat chases the fat mouse.

3. *Whose Baby Are You?* by Debby Slier. The board book is split in half and the toddler matches each familiar object with its mate; the baby with the mother and father, the chick with the hen, the kittens with the cat, the piglet with the pig, etc. The words are on the left and the toddler has to match the photographs on the right. It is also color-coded so that the words for each natural grouping are on backgrounds of the same color: chick and hen are on a tan background; kittens and cat are on a green background, etc.

4. *More, More, More Said the Baby* by Vera B. Williams. Three short episodes about three babies—Little Guy, Little Pumpkin and Little Bird. Little Guy is loved by his father who throws him up and swings him around and eventually kisses him right in the middle of his belly button. "More, more, more," laughs Little Guy. Little Pumpkin is loved by her grandmother who catches her and swings her around and kisses her toes. Little Bird's mother catches her, rocks her, gets her ready for bed and kisses her right on each of her little eyes. All the babies want more of this loving fun. Read just one episode in the group and then have parents take the book home and read the other two.

5. *I Touch* by Rachel Isadora. A toddler touches all kinds of familiar things such as the cat who is soft, a newspaper that crinkles, Daddy's beard which is scratchy, the lollipop which is sticky, the soap bubble that pops, etc. You can extend this book by having soft, hard, sticky, furry, rough, etc. objects around that the toddler can identify and touch. Toddlers love to handle everything in sight. There are two companion books to *I Touch* which are *I See* and *I Hear*. They are equally good.

II. Records

1. *Everything Grows* by Raffi. Song: "Bathtime." The toddlers pretend to take a bath and they scrub and rub themselves to a very catchy tune. You can repeat "Cleano" by Woody Guthrie which was used in Program 2 of Toddler I, if you like. Here the toddlers also pretend to take a bath. This is one activity that they all like.

2. *Can a Cherry Pie Wave Goodbye?* by Hap Palmer. Song: "Let's All Clap Our Hands Together." This is a real activity record where the toddlers can clap, shake, bounce, swing, sway, hop and jump to a very catchy tune. It doesn't really matter too much if they don't follow you or the record because they manage to do a great deal of movement and have a lot of fun with a maximum amount of giggling. They will be especially amused if you make mistakes and goof it up.

III. Film: *One Was Johnny* (3 minutes) from the animated film *Really Rosie* and based on the book *One Was Johnny* by Maurice Sendak. This is a counting story about the nine animals that come to visit Johnny who lives by himself. He decides they are much too noisy and counts backwards and gets rid of all of them and ends up being by himself again and liking the situation. This is an important point to discuss with parents as toddlers should be encouraged to do independent play. There can't always be somebody around amusing them. Another wonderful example of this independent play is the book *I'm the King of the Castle* by Shiego Watanabe. The enterprising bear in the story has a wonderful time playing by himself.

IV. Bathtub Toys. Water play is very relaxing for young children. These are toys to be taken home for play.

1. Fun Buckets (Galt). Three buckets: the first has two pour spouts; the second streams water through the holes in its side; and the third has holes in its bottom.

2. Froggie's Fleet (Discovery). Froggie has four plastic wa-
tertight boats that fit in each other or can float separately.
3. Rocking Ducks (Hand in Hand). This toy attaches to
the side of the tub with suction cups. The ducks rock
back and forth as you pour the water in the top.
4. Water Wheels (Galt). The water trickles through the
top part causing the wheel to revolve. The toy has
suction cups which attach the water wheel to the bathtub.
5. Waterpump (Childcraft). Pump the handle and see water
rush up the transparent tube and out the spout.
6. Water Activities (Ambi). A companion toy to Ambi's
Active Baby (see p. 30 and p. 102). These are four little
toys that a child can play with in the tub.
7. Watering Can (Galt). Toddlers love to fill this up and
pour the water out of it.
8. Bath Duck (Ambi). A floating yellow duck.
9. Baby Boat (Ambi). A plastic boat that children can
push in the water.

These are just eight of the toddler programs that have been
used successfully at the Farmington Library over the past several
years. You can use them as they are, or as models for programs
you build yourself. You can modify them to fit the needs of your
group, or the needs of your budget. For instance, if multiple
copies of books are a problem, you could photocopy nursery
rhymes or fingerplays. The toddler's love of repetition is a great
boon to strained budgets as well. You can cut the number of
books read by using the same books week after week—the
children love the repetition and even look forward to it. Then
you could display single copies of the other books mentioned
here for at-home use—or keep a cache of paperbacks that do not
circulate for programming use only. See page 42 for materials for
libraries with limited resources.

The point is really that the parent should not go home empty-handed, for your goal is always to encourage caregivers to do the same sorts of activities at home that you do in the library. Most of all, remember that your role is that of facilitator: your job is to keep parent and toddler attention on each other, and that is all the easier to do if you can relax and have fun with these charming little individuals and their parents.

4

Programs for Two-Year-Olds

The two-year-old program continues in the same format as Toddler I and Toddler II. Again, there is orientation, multiple copies of books, films, records, puppets and musical instruments, and, of course, involvement of the parents and caregivers. However, two-year-olds are developing control of finger and hand muscles, and are ready to start experimenting with art materials. Therefore, you need to block out an hour for this program to add an art project or another activity at the end.

Naturally, it is important to understand the basics of children's psychological development in order to design the program to cater to their needs. Two-year-olds are more interested in playing with other children than are toddlers, but because they still do not share very well, much of their play is parallel play. They are in Erik Erikson's "autonomy vs self-doubt" stage (discussed in chapter 2) and are always in conflict with themselves. One minute they are very confident, the next full of uncertainty. They also have great mood swings—very happy one moment and down in the dumps the next. You must keep in mind that they are soaking up all kinds of experiences and rapidly developing language skills at this stage. Their attention span is still short and, like the toddler, they are constantly in motion.

The following are actual programs for two-year-olds and two-and-a-half-year-olds and their caregivers. They do not have specific themes, but do tend to use materials that relate to each other. For instance, in one program the children make a fish puppet (the use of puppets is strongly encouraged throughout), and *Where's the Fish?* by Taro Gomi is read, but so is *Freight Train* by Donald Crews, because it has some of the best illustrations of movement found in children's books. The program idea is to get the children to transpose this feeling of movement to their puppet fish as they are making them. Holiday themes may seem appealing but children this age are much too young to understand and are, in fact, often frightened by masks and costumes.

There can be a lot of repetition from the toddler programs, as children like what is familiar to them. Repetition is important, so you should encourage the parents to use the same book over and over again. Do this in your program occasionally to show the parents how much the children like this re-reading. Again, display a variety of materials and talk about new books and records. Give out booklists for each program so parents can readily find the books, and if you have multiple copies, they can take them right out. It takes some parents a while to learn how to choose books for the appropriate age, so they really appreciate it when the materials are already displayed. Last of all, you can begin to use films with real people and animals in them such as *Big Red Barn* or *A Boy, a Dog and a Frog*, but most films should be animated.

Again I am going to quote *Early Childhood Literature Sharing Programs in Libraries* by Ann D. Carlson. Although all her points are relevant, I would like to highlight—from her section on storytime for children twenty-five months to thirty-six months old—three ideas that are especially relevant in running a two-year-old program (p. 39–45).

1. Parents/caregivers should be encouraged to actively participate in the activities presented during the storytime, such as fingerplays and songs, because parents/caregivers serve as models for their children. In addition, parents/caregivers are able to present follow-up activities and repeat portions

of the storytime since children enjoy the repetition of stories and activities.

This is an important point to bring up at orientation when the parents are solo and more or less have to participate in the songs and records you are doing. Repetition is also vital. I always tell parents that I could do exactly the same program every week and each child would be happy. However, since this program is geared as much to the parent as to the child, you need to introduce a variety of materials to the adults that they can use later with their children.

2. Parents/caregivers should be provided with details about the books and activities, such as booklists or printed handouts of fingerplays, poems, etc., either before or following the storytime so that the stories and activities can be repeated with the children later.

Participation is much greater when you hand out copies of fingerplays and songs. Also, the parents will want booklists and record lists and toy lists so that they can follow through after the program is over.

3. The same librarian should conduct successive storytimes so that the children can associate a person with a location.

It can be a slow process for the children's librarian to get a reaction from the child two years old and under. Many of the children will be interacting initially with an adult they do not know. When a rapport is established with the children's librarian, it should be the same librarian every week.

ADVERTISING THE PROGRAM

The two-year-old story hour is different from the usual story hour that you offer children ages three to five. If you have never offered one in your library, you need to send a flyer or write a letter to prospective parents explaining what you are starting.

An announcement in the local paper or in the Friends of the Library newsletter will help, too. In our library we keep a notebook in the children's room so parents can sign up to receive any information we may be sending out—and we have schedules available for pick-up as well. Other prime places to leave flyers are in the offices of local pediatricians, in well-baby clinics, and in daycare facilities.

Make your program schedule out at least two months before the programs are to begin so parents can plan for this activity in their busy lives. Sign-ups can be three weeks before the program is due to start, and the orientation night can be conducted one week prior to the program's beginning. We hold one of our two-year-old story hours in the evening so working parents can come. As children should not be kept out late, we schedule this from 6:30 to 7:30 P.M.

No matter how you choose to advertise your program—flyer or letter form—here is the information you will need to include.

Sample Letter

July 29, 1992

Dear Parent:

The Farmington Library is embarking on a pilot program for parents and their two-year-olds.

Both parents and children are invited to participate together in a series of short program meetings. This is meant to be a special time for you and your child to share a variety of experiences on a one-to-one basis. You and your child will play using books, toys, music, and finger-plays. Because each child's needs are varied and individual, every child will not necessarily listen to, or participate in, every activity—but relax! This is an opportunity for lots of parent-child participation.

The program starts Tuesday, September 29, from 10:00 to 11:00 A.M. and runs for seven weeks. Orientation *for parents only* is Tuesday, September 22, at 7:00 P.M. in the children's room of the Farmington Library. Sign-ups for this program begin Tuesday, September 8, at 9:00 A.M. in person, and 10:00 A.M. by phone. The telephone number of the library is 673-6291.

We hope to see you!

Sincerely,
(Your name)

SAMPLE PROGRAMS

𝕭 Two-Year-Old First Program

I. Multiple copies of books to read aloud
(20 minutes)

1. *The Very Hungry Caterpillar* by Eric Carle. This book is a goldmine of all kinds of concepts including small and big, numbers, growth, etc. Delicious things to eat are featured, and there are forty small holes in the pages for tiny fingers to go into. Introduce this book to two-year-olds, but you will find that children up to seven still enjoy it.

2. *What's for Lunch?* by Eric Carle. A monkey swings through the book looking for a fruit he likes.

3. *The Carrot Seed* by Ruth Krauss. A little boy plants a carrot seed that finally comes up just as he knew that it would.

4. *Tan Tan's Hat* by Kazuo Iwamura. Tan Tan does many tricks with his hat. He can toss and spin it and throw his hat up in the air. He catches all kinds of objects with his hat such as a grasshopper, a dog, an acorn, and a bird. Finally he throws it up in the air and catches a star.

5. *The Snowy Day* by Ezra Jack Keats. Peter, alone, explores a snowy new world that responds to his actions. He takes a stick and smacks a snow-covered tree and the snow falls on top of his head. He makes a smiling snowman and he makes angels and he climbs up a mountain of snow and slides all the way down. This book is beautifully illustrated. The two-year-old child can pick this book up and understand what's going on without knowing how to read.

II. Records and fingerplays (10 minutes)

1. *Getting to Know Myself* by Hap Palmer. Song: "Sammy." Sammy pretends to fly like a bird, swim like a fish, hop like a rabbit and crawl like a turtle. In the end Sammy sings, "I'm glad I'm me and I'm walking to the store." It is important to point out to parents that children cannot learn unless they are glad to be who they are, which is the basis of a good sense of self. This is an action song, so the children can move around (which they are ready for after listening to four or five books).

2. *If You Are Happy and You Know It Sing Along with Bob, Volume I* by Bob McGrath. Song: "Where Is Thumbkin?" It is nice to combine this fingerplay song with the action song above. The children learn what each of their fingers is called, beginning with their thumbs.

III. Film: *The Snowy Day* (6 minutes). Beautiful visual film based on the book by Ezra Jack Keats. The book and film will mean more to the child who has already experienced snow. This silent world of a city snow and a small boy's solitary delight in it have been faithfully transposed from the book.

IV. Activity: Fruit Workshop (5–10 minutes). Use the book *An Apple Is Red* by Nancy Curry before you start the fruit workshop. Assemble the parents and children around one or two tables and give them napkins and paper plates. Start with an apple and show them the difference between a peeled apple and an un-peeled apple; then an orange and an unpeeled orange; and then a banana and an unpeeled banana. Then proceed with grapes, raisins, and lemons, as illustrated in the book. Pass the cut-up fruit around to the children and have them taste and feel and smell the apples, raisins, oranges, bananas, grapes, and lemons. Then try to get them to do this with their eyes shut. Talk about the two fruit books you read in the beginning and see if the children can remember the fruits in *The Very Hungry Caterpillar* and what fruit the monkey liked best in *What's for Lunch?* This is a sensory experience for the children, and you are showing the parents how to help their children develop other senses besides the visual one.

V. **Toys** (10–15 minutes). Use plastic fruits and vegetables with the children. See if they can identify all the ones you have (there might be many more than what you used in the fruit workshop). Talk about any fruits they might not know. You can also use fruit and vegetable puzzles.

✁ Two-Year-Old Second Program

I. **Multiple copies of books to read aloud**

1. *Where's the Fish?* by Taro Gomi. Children try to find the small pink fish that has leaped out of his bowl.

2. *Freight Train* by Donald Crews. The freight train moves, really moves, going to many exciting places.

3. *I Spy at the Zoo* by Maureen Roffey. Young children will spot their favorite animals at the zoo. This is great for visual discrimination.

4. *Guess Who?* by Pam Ayres. These playful rhymes give children the chance to guess the right answer, and also provide a lot of interaction between parent and child.

5. *Whose Mouse Are You?* by Robert Kraus. The book is vast and deep in emotional content but simple in presenta-

tion. The illustration of the father and son racing around the cheeses is a great example of father-son love, as is the mother-son love in the picture of the mother mouse giving cheese to her son. At the end of the story there is a brand new baby mouse.

II. Records and fingerplays

1. *Learning Basic Skills Through Music, Volume I* by Hap Palmer. Song: "Put Your Hands in the Air." An action song to get children moving after the books have been read. Again, this emphasizes using the large muscle groups of the body.

2. *And One and Two* by Ella Jenkins. Song: "And One and Two." There are three components in this record: the counting (which you needn't stress with two-year-olds); the two different rhythms; and pointing out body parts. The children will naturally follow you during this record, although it is usually a little harder to get the parents to participate.

III. Film: *Swimmy* (6 minutes). Based on *Swimmy* by Leo Lionni. Slow and gentle movements of fish in the wonder world of the sea. (Two-year-olds will probably not understand the plot).

IV. Activity: Make a fish puppet with lots of feeling of movement based on the book *Freight Train* and the film *Swimmy*. Give the children a fish already made out of construction paper and let them decorate it any way they want. Give them crayons to color their fish. Then hand out lots of small cut-up pieces of construction paper and tissue paper strips cut in twelve-inch lengths to paste on the fish. The tissue paper strips will give the fish a feeling of movement. Next, staple on a cardboard stick to turn the fish into a rod puppet. For many children this will be the first time they have used paste, and parents are always surprised how much the children enjoy pasting. Occasionally

there will be a child who doesn't like to stick his hands in the paste so we hand him a tongue depressor to spread it on. Using puppets brings out the shy child and causes all children to verbalize more. They also have something to take home and share.

V. Follow-up Activity: The children use their fish rod puppets in the puppet theater. If you don't have a puppet theater, improvise with a sheet over a couple of straight back chairs or buy a very simple inexpensive cardboard theater. Even boxes taped together will do. The children also play with body puppets and hand puppets. Not all children can occupy the puppet theater, so you can put out the game Lottino. This is one of the first matching games for children. There are six small cardboards which are divided into different categories: one board is toys; one is kitchen utensils; one is furniture; one is animals; one is fruits; and the last board is clothing. On each board are nine different pictures and there are fifty-four pieces to match these pictures. Lottino teaches the children visual discrimination.

🎨 Two-Year-Old Third Program

I.   Multiple copies of books to read aloud

All of these deal with rhythm. The children love the flow of the language.

1. *Sheep in a Jeep* by Nancy Shaw. A jolly tale of rollicking sheep in a jeep.
2. *Jamberry* by Bruce Degan. A boy and a bear dance through a fantastic world of berries.
3. *Each Peach Pear Plum* by Janet and Allan Ahlberg. "In this book with your little eye, take a look and play 'I Spy.' " The children can find familiar nursery characters hiding in the colorful pictures. On the first page it is hard to find Tom Thumb but then you turn the page and find him quite easily; then you try to find Mother

Hubbard, and so on throughout the book. Children can soon "read" this book by themselves.

4. *The Complete Story of the Three Blind Mice* by John Ivimeny, illustrated by Paul Galdone. Galdone's dramatic illustrations recreate this classic nursery rhyme.

5. *Trot Trot to Boston* by Carol F. Ra. A group of fingerplays that are fun to do.

II. Records. Most of the children will know these songs and sing along with both records.

1. *Early Early Childhood Songs* by Ella Jenkins. Song: "Mary Had a Little Lamb."

2. *Singable Songs for the Very Young* by Raffi. Song: "Baa Baa Black Sheep."

III. Film: *The Three Little Pigs* (9 minutes). Some children may find this scary so you can try it with older two-year-olds. You need to know what the children can handle. You can introduce the movie with puppets or tell some of the story first. Children love the film but the wolf is scary.

Use *Rosie's Walk* (5 minutes) for younger twos, based on *Rosie's Walk* by Pat Hutchins. Rosie the hen goes for a walk around the farm yard. Right behind is the fox who is trying to catch up to her. Rosie has a very uneventful walk but the fox gets into all kinds of difficulties. The animation is delightful, but it is the American folk tune "Turkey in the Straw" that captivates children.

IV. Activity: Musical Instruments. Use instruments with the record *Mod Marches* by Hap Palmer. The songs "It's a Small World" and "Let It Be" work especially well.

🎜 Two-Year-Old Fourth Program

I. Multiple copies of books to read aloud

1. *Fancy That!* by Pamela Allen. The story of a hardworking red hen who hatched six fluffy yellow chicks in the company of three skeptical white leghorns. Fancy that!

2. *Old MacDonald Had a Farm* by Nancy Hellen. Ordinary farm objects turn into MacDonald's animals as the reader turns the pages of this innovative cut-out picture book. A barrel becomes a pig, a basket becomes a hen, and a haystack becomes a sheep, etc.

3. *The Box with Red Wheels* by Maud and Miska Petersham. An enchanting picture book about a strange-looking box with red wheels which is sitting in the garden. All the animals come up to the box to see what it is and make their appropriate sounds. The two-year-olds try to guess what is in the box. Originally published in 1949, this is still a great favorite.

4. *Where Is Clifford?* by Norman Bridwell. A lift-the-flap book that introduces children to Clifford, America's biggest, reddest, most loved dog. Lift the flaps and look for Clifford in the fire station, the barn, etc., until he is found in his dog house.

II. Records

1. *Activity Songs for Kids* by Marcia Berman. Song: "Farm Song."

2. *More Music for 1's and 2's* by Tom Glazer. Song: "I Had a Little Rooster."

III. Film: *The Napping House* (5 minutes). This film is based on the book by Audrey and Don Wood. Children love the repetition as they are invited to join in describing the wakeful flea on a slumbering mouse, on a snoozing cat, on a dreaming child, on a snoring Grandma—all on top of a sagging bed. Naturally they all fall down in the end.

IV. Activity: With the song "Old MacDonald Had a Farm" from the record *If You're Happy and You Know It Sing Along with Bob, Volume 2* by Bob McGrath, use hand puppets for the animals—cow, duck, dog, and pig. Make up other verses with the children for sheep, horses, goats, etc.

V. Toys

1. Little People Farm (Fisher Price). A twenty-two piece playset. It includes a barn, silo, farm equipment and animals and people with movable parts. All the pieces store inside the portable barn with carrying handle.

2. Rubber Farm Animals (Childcraft). This set includes seven animals: bull, cow, calf, horse, colt, pig and sheep. The largest animal is the horse which stands 6½" high.

3. Big Wooden Barn (Kaplan). This two-story barn measures 10¾" x 24" long and 19" wide. There are two large loft door openings and four door openings. The roof lifts up so children can move the farm animals in and out.

Two-and-a-Half-Year-Old First Program

I. Multiple copies of books to read aloud

1. *Sebastian* by Vanessa Julian-Ottie. A peek-a-boo book with the little cat Sebastian making all kinds of discoveries.

2. *Brown Bear, Brown Bear, What Do You See?* by Bill Martin, Jr. Most children are now able to identify the different colors of the animals.

3. *Big Red Barn* by Margaret Wise Brown. A lovely new edition of an old favorite. This book tells about the animals who all live together in the big red barn. It takes them through a day when the animals wake up, play, and finally go back to sleep.

4. *Henry's Busy Day* by Rod Campbell. This is a feel-book about a very busy dog. In the last illustration, when Henry finally goes to sleep in his basket, he has a soft

furry coat which the children can stroke. Children like the tactile experience.

5. *Is It Rough? Is It Smooth? Is It Shiny?* by Tana Hoban. Children can explore the textures in this book. All the objects are textured—they are rough like the tree trunk, smooth like an apple, shiny like a penny, sticky like the cotton candy, etc. You can also collect some of the objects represented here and pass them around so the children can have a hands-on experience.

II. Records

1. *You'll Sing a Song and I'll Sing a Song* by Ella Jenkins. Song: "Did You Feed My Cow?" Children are asked a series of questions such as "Did you feed my cow?" "What did you feed her?" "Did you milk her?" "How did you milk her?" etc. Ella gives the children all the answers and they recite them back to her in rhythm. Some of the answers require physical movement such as milking the cow so the child pretends to milk the cow by hand.

2. *Toddlers on Parade* by Carol Hammett. Song: "Little Bunny Foo-Foo." This activity may be used as a fingerplay. Hold the left hand out and use the first two fingers of the right hand to represent Bunny Foo-Foo as he runs, jumps, walks through the forest and then scoots home.

III. Film: *Big Red Barn* (10 minutes). Photographs of real live animals doing real live animal things. This is one of the first live action films to show older twos and it promotes much delight and interaction. Suggest to parents that they take children to see live farm animals, if at all possible.

IV. Activity: *Feel Book.* Give children a piece of construction paper folded in half to make a book. Have ready different kinds of objects that have interesting textures and are easy to attach to the book, such as scraps of fabrics, dry pasta, bits of straw, cotton balls, little pine cones, straws, aluminum foil, pieces of bark, etc. Then encourage them to paste these into their feel book. Give out crayons so the parents can write their child's name on the book and the children can color on the books. Suggest to the parents that they find other objects at home for the child to add to the book.

🎵 Two-and-a-Half-Year-Old Second Program

I. **Multiple copies of books to read aloud**

1. *Birthday Card, Where Are You?* by Harriet Ziefert. Lift the flaps and watch what happens to the birthday card that Sam sends to Sally.

2. *Big Red Bus* by Ethel and Leonard Kessler. Lots of action and sounds in this old favorite: the coins go clink, the horn goes beep, the motor roars, the wheels go round, you bounce in your seat, etc.

3. *The Bus Stop* by Nancy Hellen. Everyone is waiting for the bus to come.

4. *Truck* by Donald Crews. A large red truck is moving in a world of heavy traffic and graphic signs. It is a game to find the truck on each page. This book bursts with vitality.

5. *Color Dance* by Ann Jonas. Watch the dancers as they take five scarves, red, yellow, blue, black and white and make all kinds of color combinations from them. You can demonstrate this by using actual colored scarves with the children or using a tri-color viewer. The large (6″) transparent plastic paddles in red, yellow and blue can be combined in the viewer to make different colors. At this age the children are very interested in color and can identify the colors.

II. **Records**

1. *Songs to Grow On* by Woody Guthrie. Song: "Car Song." Pretend to go on a car trip with the children sitting on

the floor and make delightful sounds like clickety-clack, chug chug, toot toot, etc. This record makes a nice contrast to the animal sounds you've been doing.

2. *More Songs About Me* by William Janiak. Song: "If You Have This On, Stand Up." This record deals with parts of the body, clothing the child has on, and making vowel sounds. The child has to listen carefully to stand up at the right time and to make the right vowel sound. This helps develop their listening skills.

3. *I'm Not Small* by Patty Zeitlin. Song: "Coffee Grows on White Oak Trees." Introduction to a very simple circle game that can also be played at birthday parties. The children pick a partner (usually their caregiver) and dance around, then sit down, then do the whole activity over again.

III. Film: *A Boy, a Dog, and a Frog* (10 minutes). This film is based on the book by Mercer Mayer. It is another live action film which is wordless but uses classical background music.

IV. Toys: Stop Light and Safety Signs (Childcraft). These are big toys about four feet high and the stop light has batteries so the children can turn it from red to yellow to green. Also, we use airplanes, trains, trucks, cars and a town playmat. The latter is a heavy-duty vinyl mat which depicts streets in a small community. The wooden and vinyl toys and mat are from Childcraft.

🦫 Two-and-a-Half-Year-Old Third Program

I. Multiple copies of books to read aloud

1. *Winifred's New Bed* by Lyn and Richard Howell. Shows a nice transition for a child from a crib to a big bed. One of the few books that explains this to the child that may be making this switch.

2. *Who Sank the Boat?* by Pamela Allen. A hilarious picture book that always delights children. A cow, a donkey, a sheep, a pig and a tiny little mouse decide to go for a row in the bay. As each one jumps in the boat, you ask the children, "Do you know who sank the boat?" All the animals balance in the boat until the little mouse jumps in and he sinks the boat.

3. *Sam Who Never Forgets* by Eve Rice. Children are very reassured when this book is read to them. Most children want to be taken care of and do not want to be forgotten. The child will see the elephant as himself and will see Sam, the zookeeper, as the parent who has not forgotten him.

4. *When We Went to the Park* by Shirley Hughes. For an enchanting toddler and her Grandpa, a walk in the park turns into a counting game. This is a nice way to teach numbers.

5. *I Know About Shapes* by Dick Bruna. This is a first book for introducing three basic shapes.

II. Records

1. *I'm Not Small* by Patty Zeitlin. Song: "I'm Not Small." A real action record that has the child hopping like a kangaroo, crawling like a turtle, galloping like a horse, etc.

2. *Learning Basic Skills Through Music, Volume I* by Hap Palmer. Song: "Triangles, Circles and Squares." We give out a copy of the song to the parents and hope they will sing along with Hap. Also, we give out three basic shapes made out of construction paper to the children so they can hold up the right shape, at the right time in the record. Make all the shapes the same color so children are only dealing with the concept of shape. Shape is the first concept they can identify. Play the record twice—the children will like to do it again.

III. Film: *Pierre* (6 minutes). From the animated film *Really Rosie* and based on the book *Pierre* from the *Nutshell Library* by Maurice Sendak. Pierre is a little boy who doesn't care about anything. His parents are at their wits' end. One day a lion comes to call and wants to eat Pierre, and does, because Pierre doesn't care. However, everything comes out all right in the end, and Pierre does learn to care.

IV. Activity: Use big foam shapes and the song "Shapes in Action" from the record *Shapes in Action* by Georgiana Stewart. Play this record twice, as the children enjoy handling the big foam shapes so much. The foam shapes can be ordered from Kimbo Educational along with the record. The shapes are colorful and are made of fire retardant, non-toxic urethane. There are six foam shapes with pop-out centers.

V. Toys: Shape puzzles and shape toys. There are many different kinds of shape toys at many different levels of sophistication. Although children may be about the same chronological age, their developmental level can be almost a year apart in this activity. Some of the shape toys we use are Shape Board by Galt; Hippo Shape Sorter by Kiddicraft; Shape Puzzle by Salco; and Shape Beanbags by Teaching Resources. Some shape books for parents to use with children as follow-up are *My Very First Book of Shapes* by Eric Carle; *Shapes* by John J. Reiss; *Shapes and Things* by Tana Hoban; and *Round and Round and Round* by Tana Hoban, which deals only with the circle.

🦒 Two-and-a-Half-Year-Old Fourth Program

I. Multiple copies of books to read aloud

1. *Follow Me* by Nancy Tafuri. This is a beautiful wordless book about a baby sea lion who follows a red crab, and they both are followed by the mother sea lion.

2. *Eating the Alphabet* by Lois Ehlert. A colorful alphabet book that introduces young readers to a wide variety of fruits and vegetables.

3. *Of Color and Things* by Tana Hoban. A beautiful wordless book that introduces children to color and objects. One of her best!

4. *This Is the Bear and the Picnic Lunch* by Sarah Hayes. What happens when a hungry dog sneaks toward the picnic lunch just as the brave guard bear is getting a little sleepy. The dog eats the lunch but the little boy comes to the rescue and makes another picnic lunch for the three of them.

II. Records

1. *Learning Basic Skills Through Music* by Hap Palmer. Song: "Colors." Give each child a piece of construction paper—either red, green, yellow or blue—and have them all follow the actions of the song.

2. *Singable Songs for the Very Young* by Raffi. Song: "Peanut Butter Sandwich." Optional: give children peanut butter and jam sandwiches after they sing the song.

III. Film: *Alligators All Around* (2 minutes). From the animated film *Really Rosie* and based on the book *Alligators All Around* by Maurice Sendak. A family of alligators have a fun time as they rollick through the alphabet.

IV. Activities: Show and talk about alphabet books and counting books and realia. Realia are toys, articles, and other three-dimensional objects that a child handles, manipulates, or plays with to gain direct experience and information about his/her environment. Parents especially like concept books as they feel the child is really learning—but encourage them not to worry about the child learning the alphabet or numbers until she is ready. Most alphabet books and counting books are still used as object books for children this age.

Some of the books that may be discussed include *The Most Amazing Hide-and-Seek Alphabet Book* by Robert Crowther. Because this is a manipulative alphabet book, it does not last through many library circulations, so it is a great book for parents to buy. Children absolutely love it. Other similar books are *The Most Amazing Hide-and-Seek Counting Book* by Robert Crowther; *B Is for Bear* by Dick Bruna; *I Can Count* by Dick Bruna; and *Anno's Counting Book* by Mitsumasa Anno. (You can show parents *Anno's Alphabet* which is an outstanding picture book but is much too sophisticated for this age group. Show why it is not suitable for young children. Point out that some letters, like the "M", are only half there; the other half is merely a mirror image of the "D" which curves very mysteriously. The borders are very elaborate. This book is a lot of fun for older children who can figure it out.) More books to present are *A Number of Things* by Helen Oxenbury; *Teddy Bears 1 to 10* by Susanna Gretz; *Amazing Animal Alphabet Book* by Roger and Mariko Chounard; *1, 2, 3 to the Zoo* by Eric Carle; and *Ben's ABC Day* by Terry Berger.

Alphabet and number toys that are universal and made by different toy companies can be brought out for children. Examples are:

- Counting Frame. Children manipulate colorful beads on an 11" square.

- Jumbo Pegs and Pegboard. Four different colored pegs help children with counting and colors.

- Geometric Sorting Board. Sorting board with four different wood shapes. Each shape has four bright colorful pieces which children match to the correct shape and number of pegs, by fitting the piece over the wooden pegs.

- Number Worm. This curvy, red worm puzzle is self-correcting as pieces only fit together in correct sequence.

- Alpha Worm. This 36" long wriggly worm puzzle can only

be assembled in correct order. It is good for teaching letter recognition and alphabetical order.

• Wooden Alphabet Blocks. A set of twenty-eight sturdy all wood blocks with colorful letters on two sides and printed pictures and numbers on the other four sides.

• Alphabet Poster Cards. Twenty-six large 11¼" x 14" full color poster cards with upper case letters.

• Pop-up Alphabet. With this toy children simply push each lettered key to reveal a picture of an object which begins with that letter. It is made of durable plastic and measures 9" x 10".

5

Programs for Three, Four, and Five-Year-Olds

Children of three, four and five are truly on the threshold of reading, or may even be reading a few words or even simple books when they come to the library program. But not all librarians have had the good fortune to be offered instruction in reading as a process, and therefore are not always attuned to the best ways to make their programs completely successful. In the spring of 1977, the Connecticut State Library offered a federally-funded seminar series on reading explicitly for children's librarians. The all-day workshops were conducted once a week for several weeks, and were planned to meet the need all children's librarians have to understand

- How reading begins.
- What activities in the home, and in the public library, can stimulate children's interests and capabilities.
- How children's librarians can meet parents' needs to understand how reading begins, and what home activities promote reading early in the child's life.

The major objectives of the workshops were

1. To examine fundamental aspects of comprehension and learning that are applicable to the process of reading.

2. To expose librarians to a conceptual framework which they could use to make decisions in the library that would facilitate learning to read for each child.

3. To help librarians understand and respect the child's language, interests, needs, and experiences, and innate ability to learn.

4. To increase librarians' understanding of core and supportive activities for public library programs which heighten the opportunity for learning to read for all children.

5. To help librarians understand reading as a integral part of the broader communication process that includes listening, speaking, and writing.

Important things came out of this course which can be applied directly to the preschool story hour in any library. These "tips" are listed here.

1. Less formality helps the learning process. For instance, when you are taking attendance, talk to each child about what she is wearing, or on some other topic. You might have time to read one less book but the children really like being involved in a short conversation. With the three-year-old you probably will be doing most of the talking, but even if the conversation seems one-sided to you, the effect is not lost.

2. It is important to elicit responses from children all through the story hour, trying to really listen to what they say. Children must be active participants in the story hour experience to really learn from it.

3. Be prepared for the unexpected response, and be able to let children break into the story. Never be surprised at what the children might contribute. One time, in my experience, a little boy had a new baby at home. This had nothing to do with the story I was reading, but I stopped

and talked about new babies for ten minutes. You really have to do this with children ages five and under. However, you have to keep a balance so that you don't lose control of the story hour or have more than one child talking at once.

4. Place more emphasis on individual reading needs. Find out what each child is interested in and have books pre-selected that they can choose from to take home.

5. Have family story hours at night so you can get the parent more involved.

6. Repeat, repeat, repeat! It is all right for the child to like a certain book and want to read it over and over again. We have long recognized that young children (ages one to three) wanted this kind of activity but we have been hesitant to repeat it with the child ages three to five and older. We have learned that repetition is still very valid for this age group, for the child receives something more from a book each time he reads it. Yet this age is also capable of seeing a movie and reading the book in the same program and contrasting the different media.

Children's Literature in the Elementary School, 4th Edition, by Charlotte Huck, Susan Hepler, and Janet Hickman lists ten characteristics of children three, four, and five years of age that are also very helpful in planning the three, four, and five-year-old story hours. Here they are, with some more book tips based on them.

1. Rapid development of language. (Poetry books and pattern books, which are heavily repetitive, help children develop language).

2. Very active short attention span. (The three-year-old has a very short attention span, so the books and activities must be very short. Four and five-year-olds can handle longer books, especially as the year progresses. Programs for threes by themselves, and then fours and fives together, are the most successful configurations).

3. The child is the center of her own world. Interest, behavior, and thinking are egocentric. (In programs this means children like characters they can identify with).

4. The child is curious about his own world. (Encourage parents and children to get out and look for first-hand experiences; for example, going to a farm or a zoo after a story hour on zoo or farm animals).

5. The child builds concepts through many first-hand experiences. (After the experience, they can "read" books to reinforce the concepts).

6. The child has little sense of time. (Time is "before now," "now," and "not yet." One of the books I like to use to help with sequencing is *Jesse Bear, What Will You Wear?* by Nancy Carlstrom. This book takes the little bear through the day until he finally has his bath and goes to bed. Children need help with the sequencing skills that are important for reading readiness. In particular, children who look at a lot of television have very poor sequencing skills. Sequencing games and puzzles can be introduced at the end of the story hour).

7. The child learns through imaginative play and the make-believe world of talking animals and magic seems very real. (The talking animal that children seem to like best is the bear. Many of them have a bear as a stuffed animal that they take to bed so they really gravitate toward bear stories).

8. The child seeks warmth and security in relationships with the family and others. (One of the best books to give a child reassurance is *Sam Who Never Forgets* by Eve Rice. The child identifies with the elephant and thinks of Sam as his parent. This is a very comforting book).

9. The child is beginning to assert independence and takes delight in his own accomplishments. (Children want books where the young child or animal characters show initiative and independence).

10. The child makes absolute judgments about right and wrong. (Children want everything to come out all right in the end. They like books that go from order to disorder and then back to order). (Huck, p. 65–66)

PROGRAM THEMES FOR AGES THREE TO FIVE

Up to the three-year-old story hour I have listed programs that do not have specific themes but do use materials that relate to each other. I find that many children's librarians are so taken with themes that they lose sight of where the child is developmentally. For instance, in one of my two-year-old programs I have introduced the concepts of shapes with one book, one record and one activity. If, however, I had used four books on shapes, the children might not have responded. The concept of shapes could have been totally new to them and would have to be introduced to them slowly. At that age they could handle only one book on shapes. For other books in the story hour, they would like rhythm or peek-a-boo or participation books.

When children are three or older, they tend to ask for the same type of books—in other words, if you have read a scary book, they want another scary book. I have listed the next eight programs with themes because most children's librarians would like it that way. However, it is not necessary to have themes to have a successful story hour. The important thing to remember is to read good enjoyable books at the developmental level of the child and to like the books that you read yourself. Incidentally, it is much easier to find four good dog books or whatever theme you choose at the four and five-year-old level than it is to find four good dog books on the two-year-old level. If you do go with themes, make sure you pick popular topics such as birthdays, scary monsters, bears, etc. Perhaps if you have an eight-week session, you could have four story hours with themes and four story hours with more loosely related books.

PROGRAMS FOR THREE-YEAR-OLDS

For the three-year-old story hour up to fifteen children can be registered. The program can last for 45 minutes. If you do not plan a film, you probably could make the story hour 30 or 35 minutes. Sometimes you can do a short craft at the end (no more than 5 minutes). Or, instead of the craft, the child may look at the books that are displayed or play with games that are suitable for her age. The big difference from previous programs is that this story hour is held without parents. Sometimes the parents can come in at first, but are eased out after a couple of story hours. Most of the children that have been in story hour before with their parents are now very willing to be by themselves. The child who has not previously been in story hour or has not been read to much at home finds it harder to adjust. You can help to focus attention by having children sit on the carpeted floor with the storyteller on a very low chair. Such extras as story hour mats and name tags may be very distracting. The parent could be invited at the end to help with the crafts or in selecting materials to check out.

SAMPLE PROGRAMS

🎂 Three-Year-Old First Program: Birthdays

I. Attendance and interaction

II. Books

1. *Happy Birthday, Moon* by Frank Asch. A great story about friendship. The bear shares a birthday with the moon. A young child does not have to know about echoes and shadows to love this book. The young child approaches and accepts the situation just as the bear does.

2. *Benny Bakes a Cake* by Eve Rice. Benny helps Mama bake his birthday cake but Ralph, his dog, eats it up. It is Papa to the rescue with a new cake. This is a good example of a situation going from order to disorder and back to order.

3. *Happy Birthday, Sam* by Pat Hutchins. It is Sam's birthday and he is a year older. He still can't reach the light switch or the bathroom taps or the front door knob. Then his grandfather's present arrives and his problems are solved.

4. *Birthday Card, Where Are You?* by Harriet Ziefert. Lift the flaps and watch what happens to the birthday card that Sam sends to Sally. (You have to know your group. If they will let you lift the flaps and not all want to do it themselves, then you can use this book).

III. **Record:** *Happy Birthday* by Sharon, Lois and Bram. Songs: "Happy Birthday to You"; "If I Knew You Were Coming, I'd've Baked a Cake."

IV. **Activity:** Make very simple birthday cards.

V. **Film:** *Happy Birthday, Moon* (same as book).

✇ Three-Year-Old Second Program: Scary Things

Young children often have fears about monsters and scary things and nightmares, and at the same time, a fascination. The best way to deal with these fears is head on, using some of the excellent books on this subject.

I. **Attendance and interaction**

II. **Books**

1. *There's a Nightmare in My Closet* by Mercer Mayer. The boy in this book starts out being afraid of the nightmare

in his closet. However, the nightmare is such a sissy he eventually befriends him and takes him to bed.

2. *The Berenstain Bears and the Spooky Old Tree* by Stan and Jan Berenstain. Do the bears dare to go into that spooky old tree, go up that twisty old stair, go over the great sleeping bear? Yes! They dare! A great participation book—the children really enter into the actions and will do the story with you.

3. *Where the Wild Things Are* by Maurice Sendak. Max is a small boy who has been sent to bed for misbehaving. He then sails away to where the wild things are. The wild things love him and make him king, but he decides to go back to his very own room. Children identify with this book because they love Max being the boss of the wild things. All children like to be in charge of their world.

4. *Harry and the Terrible Whatzit* by Dick Gackenbach. This book deals with the common childhood fear of the unknown. Harry is sure there is something terrible in his cellar. His mother goes down there and doesn't come back up. Harry goes down to look for her and finds the terrible two-headed whatzit. His concern for his mother is greater than his fear.

III. Record: *Monsters in the Bathroom* by Bill Harley. Song: "Monsters in the Bathroom."

IV. Film: *Where the Wild Things Are* (same as book).

V. Activity: Use Max and the wild things (stuffed animals) to play at the end of the story hour. Also, bring in scary puppets to use in the puppet theater.

✿ Three-Year-Old Third Program: Food and All That Stuff

I. Attendance and interaction

II. Books

1. *Bread Bread Bread* by Ann Morris. Tantalizing photographs of bread from all over the world. Of course the bread from the United States has peanut butter and jelly on top.

2. *Sally's Secret* by Shirley Hughes. Sally likes making houses and she makes them in all sorts of places. One day she finds a very special place to make her house and invites very special people for tea.

3. *This Is the Bear and the Picnic Lunch* by Sarah Hayes. "This is the boy who packed a lunch of sandwiches, chips, and an apple to crunch. This is the bear who guarded the box while the boy went to find his shoes and his socks." Guess what happens when the bear falls asleep and the dog gets hungry—but it turns out all right in the end.

4. *The Winter Picnic* by Robert Welber. Adam plans a picnic in the snow and talks his mother into coming to it, after she realizes how important this picnic is to him.

5. *Mealtime* by Maureen Roffey. *Mealtime* is a book which encourages young children to discuss the familiar routine of eating—from what makes you hungry to your favorite foods.

III. Poems: *Poems of a Nonny Mouse* by Jack Prelutsky. "Mary Had a Little Lamb, a Lobster and Some Prunes"; "The Codfish Lays Ten Thousand Eggs"; "Baby and I Were Baked in a Pie."

IV. Record: *Singable Songs for the Very Young* by Raffi. Song: "Peanut Butter Sandwich."

V. Film: *Chicken Soup with Rice* from the animated film, *Really Rosie*, and based on the book *Chicken Soup with Rice* by Maurice Sendak.

VI. Activity: Serve bread and have children spread on peanut butter and jelly.

🐾 Three-Year-Old Fourth Program: Bear Stories

I. Attendance and interaction

II. Books

1. *Beady Bear* by Don Freeman. Beady is a fuzzy bear who belongs to a boy named Thayer. One day Thayer goes away and Beady is lost without him. Finally Thayer comes back and makes Beady the happiest bear you ever saw.

2. *My Brown Bear Barney* by Dorothy Butler. The little girl takes her brown bear Barney everywhere. Her mother says she can't take Barney to school but the little girl has other ideas.

3. *Sherwood Walks Home* by James Flora. When it begins to rain, young Robert runs home from the park, forgetting all about Sherwood, his fuzzy wind-up bear. Sherwood has many adventures trying to get home to Robert.

4. *Corduroy* by Don Freeman. Corduroy is a stuffed bear waiting in a department store for someone to buy him. One night, he embarks on a storewide search to replace a button missing from his overalls. In the morning, a little girl comes in and buys him, loves him, and replaces his button.

III. Activity: *We Are Going on a Bear Hunt* by Michael Rosen. Teach the children the actions from the book — pretending to go through grass, going through a cold river, slopping though oozy mud, etc., with the appropriate noises. When they find the bear in a cave, they quickly retreat and repeat their actions going the other way until they are home. The children pick up the actions and sounds quickly and usually like to go on a bear hunt at least a couple of times.

IV. Record: *Everything Grows* by Raffi. Song: "Teddy Bear Hug." This song tells of the relationship between a child and his teddy bear. The important thing is that the teddy bear is always there for the child giving him love and reassurance.

V. Film: *Corduroy* (same as book).

PROGRAMS FOR FOUR AND FIVE-YEAR-OLDS

For the four and five-year-old program you can handle up to twenty children. By this age they are usually very attentive when you read stories and can deal with three or four longer picture books. They enjoy the initial interaction and are eager to share their thoughts with you. Some kind of stretching activity, either a record or fingerplay or song after a couple of books, is advisable. They are still very energetic, remember!

The four and five-year-olds make a very delightful, well-behaved group that can meet anywhere. Their program lasts 45 minutes and they sit on the floor while the reader sits on a stool. With this age, as with the threes, use books that relate to each other and show films related to the books if possible. However, even with their more mature attention span, you will have to alternate books at times when they are not so attentive. These books have to be very high interest—such as the original *Curious George* books, or *Harry the Dirty Dog* books. The four and five-year-olds like to pick out their own books to take home and like to take the ones you have read. Try to have extra copies available.

SAMPLE PROGRAMS

🎄 Four and Five-Year-Old First Program: Vehicles

I. **Attendance and interaction**

II. **Books**

1. *Dear Garbage Man* by Gene Zion. Stan was a new garbage man and wanted to keep everything he collected. He threw very little into the chewer-upper at the back of the truck. He gave away all that he collected to people on his route. To Stan's surprise, the people decided they didn't want the second-hand things and gave them all back the next day. However, there is a happy ending!

2. *Dad's Car Wash* by Harry A. Sutherland. John plays hard all day with his cars and trucks. He gets very dirty. At night he visits "Dad's Car Wash"— in other words, he takes a bath! A delightful interaction between father and son.

3. *Mike Mulligan and His Steam Shovel* by Virginia Lee Burton. Mike Mulligan is faithful to his old steam shovel, Mary Anne, despite all the fancy new machines he sees. Mary Anne digs the cellar for the new town hall in one day—but then she can't get out! However, she stays there and becomes the furnace for the new town hall.

III. **Records**

1. *Songs to Grow On* by Woody Guthrie. Song: "Car Car Song."

2. *Creative Play Songs, Volume I* by Stepping Tones. Song: "The People on the Bus."

IV. Film: *The Remarkable Riderless Runaway Tricycle.* A boy's tricycle is mistakenly picked up on trash day and taken to the junkyard. Just as it is about to be crushed for scrap, the tricycle takes off and has many adventures through town.

V. Activity: Playing with cars, trucks, and all kinds of vehicles.

✄ Four and Five-Year-Old Second Program: Through the Day and Night

I.   Attendance and interaction

II.   Books

1. *Night Noises* by Mem Fox. Lily Laceby lives in an old cottage in the hills. She is almost ninety and one night she falls asleep in her chair. Then there is a lot of noise outside and all her family come in to wish her a happy birthday and give her a surprise party. "Are you really ninety?" whispers Emily, age four-and-a-half. Lily Laceby holds her hand and smiles, "Inside I'm only four-and-a-half like you," she whispers back, "but don't tell anyone."

2. *Little Fox Goes to the End of the World* by Ann Tompert. Little Fox goes to the end of the world and has many adventures on the way. Eventually she comes back to her mother, who has her favorite dinner waiting for her.

3. *The Sun's Day* by Mordicai Gerstein. The sun travels across the sky and many daily routines unfold, such as the sun coming up and eventually, after the babies take baths and go to bed, the sun going down.

4. *I Hear a Noise* by Diane Goode. It is bedtime but the little boy can't sleep and then imagines that a monster comes and steals him and his mother away. The author has taken a scary idea and turned it into a comforting bedtime story.

III. Records

1. *Everything Grows* by Raffi. Song: "Bathtime."
2. *Fun Activities for Toddlers* by Laura Johnson. Song: "You Are My Sunshine."

IV. Film: *In the Night Kitchen* by Maurice Sendak. Micky falls out of bed, out of his pajamas, down past his sleeping parents, and into the night kitchen where three Oliver Hardy-like bakers prepare to bake him a cake. Micky escapes, molds the dough into the shape of an airplane, and flies to the Milky Way to collect the milk for the cake.

✍ Four and Five-Year-Old Third Program: Scary Things

I. Attendance and interaction

II. Books

1. *Two Terrible Frights* by Jim Aylesworth. A little mouse goes to the kitchen for a bedtime snack. At the same time a little girl arrives for her snack. They scare each other and they both scamper back to bed where they are reassured by their mothers.
2. *The Gunnywolf* by A. Delaney. There once was a little girl who lived on the edge of a dark, dark woods. She didn't go into the woods because the gunnywolf lived there. One day she forgot and went into the woods to pick flowers and there was the gunnywolf. A delightful chase begins and the little girl runs for home with the gunnywolf after her, demanding that she sing the ABC song again and again. This is a great participation book as the children will sing the song every time the little girl sings it.

3. *The Spooky Eerie Night Noise* by Mona Rabun Reeve. Jenny hears a noise in the backyard and imagines a yard full of spooky possibilities. What the noise turns out to be will surprise children.

4. *The Judge* by Harve Zemach. "A horrible thing is coming this way, creeping closer day by day. Its eyes are scary, its tail is hairy. I tell you, Judge, we all better pray!" Each succeeding prisoner tells this to the judge with an added description of the approaching monster. But the judge does not believe them. It is fun to give the children paper and have them draw the monster from the description before they see it in the end, eating up the judge.

III. Activity: Repeat the ABC song from *The Gunnywolf.*

IV. Film: *The Little Girl and the Gunnywolf.* This film is the result of a project carried out by a kindergarten teacher and her pupils. The film is animated with student drawings and is narrated by the students in their own idiom. It is outstanding!

Four and Five-Year-Old Fourth Program: Friendship

I.   Attendance and interaction

II. Books

1. *Annie Bananie* by Leah Komaiko. There never was a friend quite like Annie Bananie! Then Annie Bananie has to move away and all the good time activities the two little girls did together are described in this tale of friendship.

2. *Jessica* by Kevin Henkes. This is the story of Ruthie and her imaginary friend Jessica. A very special story about the delightful gift of imagination and the warmth of first friendship.

3. *The Very Best of Friends* by Margaret Wild. James and his cat, William, are the very best of friends but Jessie, his wife, does not like William. Then James dies and Jessie does not care about anything. It is up to William to prove to her that although he can't replace James, he can be a good friend.

4. *Lizzie and Harold* by Elizabeth Winthrop. Lizzie wants a best friend more than anything else in the world so she tries to make one happen. In the end, she picks someone who has always been around and has always wanted to be her best friend.

III. Record: *We All Live Together* by Steve Millang and Greg Scelsa. Song: "We All Live Together."

IV. Film: *Frog On His Own.* Frog gets separated from his friend and has a series of funny adventures before they are reunited.

6

Choosing and Using Toys

Toys play an important part in the development of the child, and so are an important component in our library service to children. Being able to check out toys from the library can put a good educational experience into the hands of many children and introduce infants, toddlers, and even older children to a fun-filled and imaginative place—a library to which they want to return.

Playing with babies can foster in them many learning experiences such as basic trust, social interaction, body mastery, self-concept, language and cognitive development. The important thing is the interaction of adult and child and many times using toys makes the experience more rewarding.

In the parent-infant program, outlined in chapter 2, toys play an essential part. In order for young children to realize that a picture of a ball in a book is a ball, you can give them the three-dimensional "real" ball and encourage them to make the translation. Identifying objects in books in the first twelve months of life is a main delight of the youngster and it is helpful to have toys of many of the objects they see in a book.

Toys also play an important part in the toddler and two-year-

100

old programs. It is easier to teach concepts with toys. For example, the concept of roundness cannot (logically) be communicated by the printed page. In the two-year-old program we use big foam rubber shapes so the children can feel and see and understand the concept of shape.

Parents and librarians and early childhood teachers need a clearer understanding of the value of play and the kinds of playthings that support children's developmental needs. For this reason Dr. Frank Self of St. Joseph's College in Connecticut and I put together a list of selected toys for a series of workshops, "Services for the Up-to-Threes and Their Parents," for the Connecticut State Library in 1984. We have periodically updated this *List of Selected Toys for Children Under Three*. These toys have been successfully circulated by the Farmington Library for the past ten years. We hope that by writing annotations for these toys and describing how the child will probably use them, other adults will be helped in evaluating and picking out toys.

In our toy annotations we have indicated the type of cognitive process the child is experiencing when engaged in the described activity. In the following list, CPT refers to the type of cognitive process at work:

- CPT 1: CHILD INVESTIGATED WORLD. Here the child inspects and investigates the toy as an object, becoming aware of the physical attributes of the object/toy through various simple and repetitive action patterns.

- CPT 2: CHILD MAKES IMPACT ON THE WORLD. Here the child initiates actions on the toy and the toy responds in some physical way. This sequence sets up a contingency situation such that the greater the variety of responsive modes and the greater the degree of response, the greater are the degree of affect, the activity level, and the duration on the part of the child.

- CPT 3: CHILD MAKES CHANGES IN THE WORLD. Here the child initiates actions on the toy which result in changes in structure, configuration, or pattern, often along the continuum from disorder to order or order to disorder. These changes may result from the child's actions either directly, as when the child controls the subject direction, degree, and timing of the changes, or indirectly, as when the child trips a mechanism which starts the predetermined and programmed action pattern.

- CPT 4: CHILD MAKES NEW WORLDS. Here the child initiates actions on the toy in a manner which establishes a dramatic actor and co-actor interaction. This is through the creation of story form, narrative, and sometimes, plot. While higher in degree of imagination than the previous three types of cognitive processing, this dramatic play is realistic in orientation and ritualistic in form.

LIST OF SELECTED TOYS FOR CHILDREN UNDER THREE

Toys and What They Teach

ACTIVE BABY (Ambi). From ages six months to two years. This is the Mozart of baby toys, simple and beautiful objects which create a wonder of elegant complexity and harmonies (CPT 1, CPT 2, and CPT 3). Encourages discrimination of shape, sound, color; understanding of concepts of fit/not fit, cause and effect, and balance; and the development of focal attention, eye-hand coordination, motor skills, and blowing.

BABY'S FIRST CAR (Ambi). From ages six months to three years. The child can make the car go forward and backward and also can make the eyes move; the child can also press the red button and make the car squeak (CPT 2). Some children will also use this car for rather dramatic play (CPT 4). Encourages physical activity and coordination and imagination.

BABY'S FIRST FONE (Ambi). From about six months well into the third year. This toy is unusual in that at the youngest age the child will inspect and investigate it as an object (CPT 1), then shake, turn, and press its various parts, thus creating a contingency situation (CPT 2), then will take the receiver on and off (CPT 3), and finally, engage in dramatic play by listening and talking over the phone (CPT 4). Encourages discrimination of sound and the development of manual dexterity, modeling behavior, and imagination.

BUSY CLUTCH BALL (Child Guidance). From age four months to two years. At first the child will bat and kick the ball in the crib and later will finger, and then grab, the varied knobs (CPT 1). Outside the crib the "ballness" of the ball will take over, but it doesn't roll very far, it sometimes changes direction, it barely bounces at all, and it is easy to hold (CPT 2). All this is ideal for the child who is crawling and beginning to walk. Encourages development of motor coordination, focal attention, and tactile discrimination.

CATERPILLAR OSCAR (Brio). From ages one year to beyond three years. The child will begin by propelling Oscar by hand. Then, when the child is walking, a string with a sturdy knob can be attached to the two horns for pulling. Still later, the child will want more control and will go back to propelling Oscar by hand (CPT 2). Eventually it will join the car and truck as a vehicle in imaginative play (CPT 4). This toy makes children laugh.

CHATTER TELEPHONE (Fisher-Price). From age one to three years. This is a pull toy which, when pulled, sounds "chatter chatter" and the eyes roll up and down. A bell rings when a dial is turned (all CPT 2). An entertaining toy for developing physical coordination and color discrimination.

CLICK-A-WHEEL (Kiddicraft). From age six months to beyond three years. Here is a toy which is advertised as producing seven different sounds and indeed it does. The sound easiest to make is produced by shaking, but not in just any direction, so a contingency situation is created. The other sounds are produced by turning one or both knobs or holding one knob and swinging the wheel (all CPT 2). Encourages discrimination of sound, directionality, and color as well as motor coordination.

CLOTH BLOCKS (Galt). From ages four months to two years. Baby's first blocks. Six big squeezable blocks to be stacked up and knocked down (CPT 2). Encourages development of eye-hand coordination and balancing.

COGWHEEL BOARD (Brio). From age eighteen months to beyond three. This toy provides children with an experimental base for understanding a mechanical process as well as developing focal attention, motor coordination, the concept of touching/not touching, and color discrimination (CPT 2).

COLOR MOBILE, SOUND SPINNER, and SUN MUSIC BOX (Fischer-form). Ages birth to twelve months. These three crib toys are designed to hang from the Fischerform cot toy rod and the pram rod. The Color Mobile presents two clear and colorful patterns within the visual field of the supine infant, thus promoting focal attention (CPT 1). The Sound Spinner is an ingenious rattle which stimulates arm and leg activity (CP,T 2). The Sun Music Box promotes focal attention, visual scanning, and sound discrimination (CPT 2), but be sure to select a melody which is not fast or too complex.

CORNPOPPER (Fisher-Price) From age one year to three years. Walkers push this fast to enjoy the sight and sound (CPT 2). As the wheels turn on this bright push toy, colored balls jump around inside a clear cylinder and make a popping noise.

CRAWL-A-BALL (Discovery) From four months to eighteen months. This is a ball to grab, gum, and chew on (CPT 1). It rolls only a few feet and barely bounces (CPT 2). Encourages development of focal attention.

CRAWLY MIRROR (Fischerform). The second year. A toy to crawl to, push away, crawl to again, and use to look at oneself and the nearby world (CPT 2). Encourages focal attention and motor activity.

FLYING OCTOPUS (Kouvalias). From age one year to three years. This pull toy features colored balls on springs above a caterpillar. (We don't understand the name either). It makes a marvelous giddy movement when brought to rest and turns and rattles when pulled (CPT 2). Encourages discrimination of same/different, color, and the development of focal attention and motor activity.

GIANT WOODEN KNOB INSETS: Fruit and Animals (Didago).

From age two years to beyond three years. On these puzzles, the large knobs make holding easy, but the fit is tight. These toys encourage eye-hand coordination, matching, categorization, labeling, and language development while the child changes the configuration from order to disorder and back to order (CPT 3). Since each inset piece illustrates an entire fruit or animal, they will also be used for dramatic play (CPT 4).

HANDY BOXES (Ambi). From age six months to beyond three years. These six nesting boxes need to be approached as three distinct toy sets, bottoms alone, bottoms and tops, and tops alone. The youngest child will investigate the bottoms alone, eventually realizing their nesting property (CPT 1). The child from age eighteen months will use bottoms and tops as sound boxes (CPT 2), and soon after as containers to hide and store small objects and also to create various tall pyramids (CPT 3). The eighteen-month-old will begin to use the handy boxes in sand and water play as scoops, containers, and (with sand) as molds (CPT 3). At age two years the child will use them in dramatic play, especially as table service (CPT 4). Still later the tops may be nested and placed in pyramid shapes to serve as bases for small prized objects. Encourages discrimination of size and color, development of modeling behavior, understanding of the concepts of object permanency, in/out and fit/not fit.

LOTTINO (Ravensburger). From age two and one-half years to beyond three years. Although much of the value of this lotto game will only be gained by children beyond three years, older two's will enjoy the pictures and matching them (CPT 3). Encourages development of focal attention, eye-hand coordination, matching, categorization, labeling, and receptive and expressive language. Also encourages understanding of the concepts of same/different, and directionality.

POSTING BOX (Brio). From age one year to three years. Putting the differently colored and shaped pieces into the appropriate holes stimulates the child to develop focal attention, eye-hand coordination, object permanency, and also to discriminate shape and color (CPT 3).

POUNDING BENCH and HAMMER THE BEADS (Brio). From age

two years to beyond three years. Both toys help eye-hand coordination, strength, manual dexterity, color discrimination, and the understanding of tool use. Hammer the Beads is attractive and fun to use, and, since balls momentarily disappear after being hit through the colors before they roll along the bottom, it involves a bit of peek-a-boo which helps the child develop the concept of object permanency. Pounding Bench has pegs which never come out of the wood block, and it requires considerable strength, concentration, and persistence (all CPT 3).

ROCK 'N' ROLL (Ambi) From age one month to eighteen months. The rattle, rolling, and balancing provide immediate and varied response to the child's initiating action (CPT 2). This toy encourages motor activity in the crib as well as crawling on the floor.

ROLL A WHEEL (Ambi). From age one year to two years. A push toy with a "clackety-clack" sound which encourages children to walk and push (CPT 2).

SAND-WATER MILL (Discovery). From age two years to beyond three years. With this toy the child can channel sand or water and start and stop the flow (CPT 3) and in the process begin to understand the basic mechanics of the funnel, slideway door, and waterwheel. Later, with trucks and train cars, this will be used in dramatic play (CPT 4).

STACK AND DUMP TRUCK (Johnson & Johnson). From about eighteen months to beyond three years. Colored chips can be fitted over posts, on headlights, on hubcaps, and in slots in the rear cargo area of the truck (CPT 3). Encourages development of motor skills, imagination, dramatic play, and object permanency.

STACK AND POP (Discovery). From age one year to beyond three years. There are six hemispheres that fit on a pole. At the base of the pole there is a switch, so when the child threads the hemispheres on the pole and pushes them down, he then can release the switch and they all pop up (CPT 3). This makes for a safe Fourth of July year round and encourages discrimination of same/different, size, and color. The hemispheres can also enhance water play and block building.

SWISS CAR and SWISS PLANE (Naef). From age eighteen months to beyond three years. In addition to using these as vehicles in dramatic play, the child will also imitate the two faces—the car has a frown face and the plane has a smile face—and perhaps introduce feelings into the play (CPT 4).

THREADING SHAPES, SET I (Brio). From age ten months to two years. Both are a pleasure to rattle, mouthe, and teethe on (CPT 1). First with the balls, later with the cubes, they are a challenge to thread through the plastic disks. Encourages discrimination of shape and color and the development of focal attention and motor coordination.

CIRCULATING TOYS (REALIA) IN THE LIBRARY

Many libraries are now circulating toys and find them very popular with children, parents, and teachers. The Farmington Library started circulating toys in 1974 with a $100 budget. Before we started we explained on a large bulletin board in the children's room what we were doing and why we were beginning to circulate toys. This explanation can also be made at an open house or parent program. We always relied heavily on used toys from patrons. The best toys to circulate in a library are durable. Parents who buy these kinds of toys find that they outlast their child's interest and will contribute the toys to the library. Like book contributions, you have to use your own judgment whether to put them in the collection or not.

Safety is always a major consideration in introducing toys to the library. You should make sure that the toys have been checked out with the Consumer Products Safety Commission banned toy list, and keep checking that list. We have had to withdraw two toys that we purchased and circulated which, after being on the market, proved to be unsafe. One was Johnson & Johnson's Three Triplets and the other was an Ambi peek-a-boo toy. Both of these manufacturers are excellent companies and produce superior toys, but problems can always arise.

Also, the toys should be nonflammable and able to be washed

or cleaned, if necessary. The toys should be carefully checked after each circulation to make sure they are not broken or have acquired problems that make them a safety hazard. The toys should be labeled if they have small parts and are not suitable for a child under three. We do not purchase toys that go in the mouth such as harmonicas or teething rings. However, many infants will put all kinds of toys in their mouths so that is why they should be washable.

We divide our toys into five categories:

1. Realia Infant. Toys for children from birth to one year.
2. Realia Preschool. Toys for children from one year to five years.
3. Realia Elementary. Toys and games for children from six to nine years old.
4. Realia Intermediate. Toys and games for children from ten to thirteen.
5. Realia Junior High. Games for junior high ages.

We circulate most of our toys in Monaco plastic bags which come in eight sizes. The larger toys we circulate in mesh bags which come in two sizes. We have a label which is laminated and fastened to the bag, i.e.:

REALIA PRESCHOOL FL   (*Farmington Library*)

Goula   (*manufacturer*)

Insertible Super Silhouettes Shape
Stacker   (*title*)

32501 04480 8680   (*bar code number*)

We have a card taped inside the bag which reads:

REALIA PRESCHOOL

Goula

Insertible Super Silhouettes Shape Stacker

32501 04480 8680

14 pieces, 1 board   (*all the pieces would have FL +*
                            32501 04480 8680 on the back)

Once you make toys a basic part of programming, parents, teachers, and others who work with children will ask for recommendations about which to check out from the library, or even to purchase. Many toys will last several years, while the child will tire of others the minute he masters the skill involved. An example of the former is blocks and of the latter is the simple puzzle. Blocks keep the interest of children for many years, and are therefore a good toy for parents to purchase. Puzzles, on the other hand, are the perfect toys to check out of the library.

We make lists of toys for parents to purchase for each age, and of course many of the toys are on several lists. We update these lists once a year to incorporate purchases by the library. The library staff encourages parents to borrow a toy from the children's department that they are thinking of purchasing. While toys may be suitable, children may not like them—and as good toys are expensive, parents should gauge a child's interest before buying.

The programs in chapters 2, 3, and 4 in particular show how toys can be used with books, to reinforce them, and to illuminate their meaning for young children or to lead into crafts or other projects. Toys become the child's tools by which she can try out the ideas presented to her in the book and in life. There are lots of "for instances": children who have had *Animal Sounds* by Aurelius Battaglia read to them love to play with farm animal puppets or vinyl farm animals, while they repeat the gobbles, growls, and grunts of the animals. The same is true when toys are tied into films, such as *Big Red Barn*, itself based on the book by Margaret Wise Brown. The farm animals (real ones) shown in this film can lead directly into puppet and toy play, and can lead out again, too: to a real barnyard or children's zoo where the parent could take the child, or even to a pet at home (but only if the child is old enough to help take care of it).

Toy vehicles, traffic signs, and motor mats go well with such books as *Truck* and *Freight Train* by Donald Crews, or *Fire Engine* and *Big Wheels* by Anne Rockwell. Musical instruments, hats, tools—there are a wealth of possibilities for tie-ins. For the under-threes it is best to follow the book with the toy, but older children will not be distracted by hearing the book, such as *Mike Mulligan and His Steam Shovel* by Virgina Lee Burton, while you present the toy steam shovel simultaneously. Many books can be toys in themselves—all the peek-a-boos, for example—such as *Where's Spot?* by Eric Hill. In this book the child is necessary to complete the action of the book (which makes it a perfect CPT 2 toy).

Blocks play an important part in our programs. We constantly say to parents, "If you are only going to buy your child one toy, make it blocks." We circulate many kinds of them and we play with several types in the library programs. At the end of programs we usually hand out the chart on blocks from *The Block Book* edited by Elizabeth S. Hirsch, which shows all the different kinds of learning resulting from block play. Some of the building books that we use with blocks and cardboard boxes are *I Can Build a House* by Shiego Watanabe, *Block City* by Robert Louis Stevenson, *Building a House* by Byron Barton, *Beep Beep, I'm a Jeep* by Felice Haus, and *Baby in a Box* by Frank Asch. The film *Changes, Changes* based on the book by Pat Hutchins adds to the delight of children as they watch different things being built with blocks in the film.

The following lists of match-ups of toys with books, films, records or tapes, are a handy and quick set of look-up guides for those starting toy programs. Many of these are included in the sample programs in earlier chapters, and others are here for you to build on.

TOYS TIED IN WITH BOOKS

Toy	Book
Bubble wand Bubble pipe	*Bubbles* by Mercer Mayer
Feely bag (a bag full of objects which the child tries to identify by feel)	*Misty's Mischief* by Rod Campbell *Is It Rough? Is It Smooth? Is It Shiny?* by Tana Hoban
Jumbo touch and match Texture dominoes	*Buster's Bedtime* by Rod Campbell *The Very Busy Spider* by Eric Carle
Dinosaur puppets and figures	*Dinosaurs, Dinosaurs* by Byron Barton
Foam shapes	*Shapes* by John Reiss *I Know About Shapes* by Dick Bruna *Round and Round and Round* by Tana Hoban
Safety signs	*I Read Symbols, I Read Signs* by Tana Hoban

Toy	Book
Picnic sets	*This Is the Bear and the Picnic Lunch* by Sarah Hayes *The Winter Picnic* by Robert Welber *Picnic* by Emily A. McCully
Mother Goose figures	*Each Peach Pear Plum* by Janet and Allan Ahlberg *The Great Big Book of Nursery Rhymes* by Peggy Blakely *The Real Mother Goose* by Blanche Fisher Wright
Noah's Ark	*Noah's Ark* by Peter Spier *Noah's Ark* by Jenny Thorne *Noah's Ark* by Nonny Hogrogian *Noah and the Great Flood* by Warwick Hutton
Farm animals	*Teddy Bear Farmer* by Phoebe & John Worthington
Farm	*Big Red Barn* by Margaret Wise Brown
Farm animal puppets	*The Box with Red Wheels* by Maud and Miska Petersham *Farm Noises* by Jane Miller *Early Morning in the Barn* by Nancy Tafuri *Good Morning, Chick* by Mirra Ginsburg *Animal Sounds* by Aurelius Battaglia

Toy	Book
	Old MacDonald Had a Farm by Glen Rounds
Zoo animal sets	*Dear Zoo* by Rod Campbell *Sam Who Never Forgets* by Eve Rice *Zoo* by Bruno Munari *1, 2, 3 to the Zoo* by Eric Carle *When We Went to the Zoo* by Jan Ormerod
Tea sets	*Sally's Secret* by Shirley Hughes
Hats	*Whose Hat?* by Margaret Miller *Look, There's My Hat* by Maureen Roffey *How Do I Put It On?* by Shigeo Watanabe *Tan Tan's Hat* by Kazuo Iwamura
Tool box	*The Tool Box* by Anne & Harlow Rockwell
Steam shovel	*Mike Mulligan and His Steam Shovel* by Virginia Lee Burton
Vehicles	*Machines at Work* by Byron Barton *Big Wheels* by Anne Rockwell *William and the Vehicle King* by Laura P. Newton *Fire Engines* by Anne Rockwell *Freight Train, Truck, and School Bus* by Donald Crews

Toy	Book
	Piggy at the Wheel by Derek Radford
Airplanes	*Airport* by Byron Barton *Planes* by Anne Rockwell
Color dominoes	*Colors* by Shirley Hughes
Color-paddles	*Color Dance* by Ann Jonas
Match-A-Color	*Mouse Paint* by Ellen Stoll Walsh
Color pattern board	*Brown Bear, Brown Bear, What Do You See?* by Bill Martin, Jr.
Alphabet teacher	*Mary Wore Her Red Dress, and Henry Wore His Green Sneakers* by Merle Peek
Match-a-balloon	*Color Zoo* by Lois Ehlert *Color* by John Reiss
Stuffed bears (There is a Corduroy bear)	*Teddy Bears Stay Indoors* by Susanna Gretz *Teddy's Ear* by Niki Daly *My Brown Bear Barney* by Dorothy Butler *Corduroy* by Don Freeman *Happy Birthday, Moon* by Frank Asch *Ask Mr. Bear* by Marjorie Flack
Stuffed animals-dogs (There is a Spot dog)	*Where's Spot?* by Eric Hill
Stuffed animals-hippo	*Hot Hippo* by Mwenye Hadithi
Play telephones	*Good Night, Fred* by Rosemary Wells

TOYS TIED IN WITH FILMS

Toy	Film
All kinds of cardboard boxes	*At Your Fingertips: Boxes.* A great movie to show both parents and children as it illustrates all the fun things that you can make out of ordinary cardboard boxes from the supermarket.
Animal farm puppets, farm animals, Fisher-Price farm	*Big Red Barn.* Photographs of real live animals doing real live things. Promotes much delight and interaction of parents and children.
Cardboard blocks, wooden blocks, foam blocks	*Changes, Changes.* Simple story of building blocks and two wooden dolls. The dolls build several different forms with the blocks. Great film for block play follow-up.
	Tchoo, Tchoo. Stop motion photography animates a city of blocks and creates adventures for children. Rollicking, rhythmic music accompanies the movements of a train, a ladybug, and a dragon made of blocks. Great for block play follow-up.
Stuffed animal: Corduroy bear	*Corduroy.* A stuffed bear waiting in a department store for someone to buy.

Toy	Film
	A *Pocket for Corduroy.* Corduroy becomes lost while at the laundromat and encounters many adventures in his effort to get back home. We also discover why he needs a pocket.
Stuffed animal or puppet: Curious George	*Curious George.* Animated film from H. A. Rey's book about the curious monkey, George, who is taken from his native jungle to the city by the man in the yellow hat.
Boa puppets	*The Day Jimmy's Boa Ate the Wash.* Jimmy brings his pet boa on the class outing. Funny things happen as a result.
Paper kites	*Fish from Japan.* Harvey, the new kid in school, is expecting a special "fish" from his uncle in Japan. When the fish that arrives is not what was expected, Harvey manages to turn the situation to his advantage and gain the respect of his classmates.
Toy cars	*Great Toy Robbery.* Animated spoof of westerns and cowboys. Santa Claus is robbed by bad men at Dry Gulch. The hero

Toy	Film
	(accidentally) captures the villains. Santa's snatched bag is returned and our hero rides off into the sunset in a toy car.
Lion puppet or stuffed animal	*The Happy Lion.* The happy lion who lives in the zoo is surprised by the unexpected public reaction when he goes into town to visit his friend.
Animal puppets for characters in the song, and one old lady doll puppet	*I Know an Old Lady Who Swallowed a Fly.* Burl Ives sings this old favorite accompanied by lively animal characters.
Puppet set: Goldilocks and the Three Bears	*Goldilocks and the Three Bears.* Goldilocks takes the short cut through the woods and straight to the house of the three bears.
Drums and musical instruments	*The Little Engine That Could.* Animated film based on the children's classic about the little engine that pulled a load of toys to the children on the far side of the mountain.
Stacking dolls and all stacking toys	*Matrioska.* A band of Russian wooden dolls, hollow and in graded sizes so that the largest holds all the rest, dance to zestful Russian music. Beautifully animated.

Toy	Film
Pig animals and puppets	*The Pigs' Wedding.* Porker and Curly Tail invite all their pig friends to the wedding, but when the guests arrive they are all in need of a bath.
All riding vehicles	*The Remarkable Riderless Runaway Tricycle.* Live action nonverbal film about a boy's tricycle mistakenly picked up on trash day and taken to the junkyard. Just as it is about to be crushed for scrap, the tricycle magically takes off and has many adventures through town.
All kinds of toys	*Santa's Toys.* Shows how the toys that Santa has left come to life and enjoy having fun on Christmas Eve.
Puppet kit of *Sylvester and the Magic Pebble*	*Sylvester and the Magic Pebble.* Sylvester, a pebble-collecting donkey, finds a magic pebble and has some interesting adventures.
Puppets of the Three Little Pigs and the Big Bad Wolf	*The Three Little Pigs.* The music, cartoons, and pace are all magnificently alive. Some adults do not like the violence but older twos and older children are entranced by the clarity of the action and the incredible energy.

Toy	Film
Stuffed animals of Max and the Wild Things	*Where the Wild Things Are.* Animation based on Sendak's Caldecott Award-winning book. Takes place in a child's imaginary world, where anything can happen and does.
Small vehicles play mat	*Alexander and the Car with the Missing Headlight.* A fantasy about a small boy's adventures around the world.
Steam shovels, bulldozers	*Mike Mulligan and His Steam Shovel.* Mike Mulligan remains faithful to his steam shovel, Mary Ann, against the threat of new gas and diesel engine contraptions, and digs his way to a surprising and happy ending.

TOYS TIED INTO RECORDS AND TAPES

Toy	Record or Tape
Five little monkeys puppet mit	"Five Little Monkeys" from *Finger Plays and Foot Plays* by Rosemary Hallum
Bus	"The Wheels on the Bus" from *Finger Plays and Foot Plays* by Rosemary Hallum

Toy	Record or Tape
Zoo animals	"Going to the Zoo" from *Singable Songs for the Very Young* by Raffi
Musical instruments	*Mod Marches* and *Homemade Band* by Hap Palmer
Cars	"Car Song" from *Songs to Grow On* by Woody Guthrie
Trains	"Puffer Bellies" from *One, Two, Three, Four, Look Who's Coming Through the Door* by Sharon, Lois and Bram
	"Rock-A-Motion Choo Choo" from *We All Live Together* by Steve Millang and Greg Scelsa
Jack-in-the-box	"Jack in the Box" from *It's Toddler Time* by Carol Hammett
Duck puppets	"Six Little Ducks" from *More Singable Songs* by Raffi
	"Little White Duck" from *Toddlers on Parade* by Carol Hammett
Bunny puppets	"Little Rabbit Foo-Foo" from *Mainly Mother Goose* by Sharon, Lois and Bram
Snakes	"Sally the Swinging Snake" from *Sally the Swinging Snake* by Hap Palmer

Toy	Record or Tape
Child's bowling set	"The Bowling Song" from *One Light One Sun* by Raffi
Shapes	"Triangle, Circle, or Square" from *Learning Basic Skills Through Music, Volume II* by Hap Palmer
	"Shapes in Action" from *Shapes in Action* by Georgiana Stewart
Farm animals	"Old MacDonald Had a Farm" from *If You're Happy and You Know It Sing Along with Bob, Volume I* by Bob McGrath
	"I Had a Little Rooster" from *More Music for One's and Two's* by Tom Glazer
Noah's Ark	"Who Built the Ark" from *If You're Happy and You Know It Sing Along with Bob, Volume I* by Bob McGrath
Boats	"Michael Row the Boat Ashore" from *Pulling Together* by Gemini
	"Tug Boats" from *Activity Songs for Kids* by Marcia Berman

For budgetary and other reasons, it may not be feasible for all libraries to purchase and circulate the toys discussed here. Yet a very good beginning collection can be assembled quickly and inexpensively—either by asking for donations in a "toy drive" or enlisting the aid of the Friends of the Library or another organization. (See Materials for Libraries with Limited Resources in chapter 3). A start-up collection of toys should adhere to the criteria for safety which is to follow, and for suitability as discussed in this chapter. It should include:

All kinds of musical
  instruments
Puppets: finger, body, hand
  and rod
Vinyl play mat
Play hats
Beads on a wire game
Cardboard boxes
Puzzles
Stuffed animals
Blocks

Big and little traffic signs
Holes and peek box
Red wagon
Large mirror
Foam shapes
Trains, trucks, airplanes and
  other vehicles
Riding vehicles
Farms
Airport

CRITERIA FOR CHOOSING TOYS

In her article "Long Live the Little Red Wagon," Judy Markey advises parents to seek out the classic toy that they grew up with for their own children rather than the teddy bear that talks back or a doll that performs three bodily functions or a talking remote car that is destined to meet a premature death. She goes on to describe some of the classic toys and how children relate to them.

> What makes building blocks or baby dolls or even messy, but marvelous, PlayDoh such enduringly wonderful toys is that the kid has to put the wonderfulness into them. These aren't toys with adorable little adoption papers, or confining directions, or pre-programmed formats. They are gimmickless toys. They trigger the imagination, provoke pretending, don't do the pretending for you. They are toys whose wonderfulness is totally dependent on fantasy, on physical exertion, on industriousness. Open a box of Tinkertoys and you can create any whatchamacallit in the world. Open a can of PlayDoh and you can squoosh its contents into the creature, castle, or handprint paperweight of your wildest dreams. (p. 166)

For those still in doubt, a sound guide for toys ran in *Learning Magazine's* November 1977 issue, listing seven suggestions for discretionary toy buying:

1. Match toy to child
2. Make sure the toy encourages, not stifles, creative and imaginative play.
3. Consider your own interest only if you intend to use the toy with the child.
4. Compare prices, shop around.
5. Is the toy safe?
6. Check assembly requirements.
7. Is the toy workable and durable and livable?

The National Association for the Education of Young Children publishes an interesting brochure entitled "Toys = Tools for Learning" to give out to parents. It has a chart that starts at birth to three months, and goes up to five and six-year-olds. It lists characteristics of children at eight stages of development and types of good toys for each group. It also has this toy shopping checklist and suggests that parents ask these questions before they buy a toy:

- Is this toy for my child's age?
- Will my child be interested enough to play with it over and over again? For several minutes or even an hour at a time?
- Is it constructed well? Will it hold up to lots of use?
- Does my child provide the power and imagination to operate the toy?
- Will my child feel successful when using the toy? Does it challenge my child's abilities just enough?
- Can the toy grow with my child? Will it still be appealing in a year? For several years?
- Can my child use the toy in different ways? Can it be used creatively?

- Will it help my child learn about other people, nature, or how things work?

These questions are really no different in kind from the concepts presented earlier in this chapter as CPTS—cognitive process types. Here, instead of applying them to child-toy interaction to foster growth, they can be used as the basis for practical and successful buying decisions. But what toys are not suitable? How do we know what is bad? One source of information here is the Reverend Christoper Rose, an Episcopal priest in Hartford, Connecticut, who targets "warped" toys on the Christmas gift market. These include toys that vomit, dolls whose eyes pop out in a spurt of fake blood, and costume kits for turning an eight-year-old into a homeless bag lady (complete with makeup to simulate a death pallor). In the *Hartford Courant* of December 2, 1990, Rose stated: "These toys have nothing to do with the spirit of Christmas. This is an insult to the season. We are supposed to be thinking in terms of being caring and generous and loving to our children. We want to make them happy. This doesn't do it. What it does is desensitize children to violence, mutilation, suffering, and pain."

Rose was particularly unhappy about a toy called Steve the Tramp, a plastic doll based on a character from the comic strip "Dick Tracy." Rose led a protest that turned into a national swell of indignation in 1990 over the appearance of the homeless tramp, described as hardened and bitter and capable of preying on the young and helpless. That particular doll has been pulled off the shelf and its production ended.

From an article in the *New York Times*, February 6, 1992, "Who believes in make believe?" comes an assertion from one of the largest toy manufacturers that "young girls want to strap onto their bellies a baby doll that creates a vivid illusion of being pregnant, with the shape, kick and heartbeat of the real thing." Little boys want to "crash cars and watch as dummies inside are thoroughly mutilated on impact, spewing arms and legs and even their heads out the window."

Two experts replied on these kinds of toys.

"These toys are going too far," said Dr. David Elkind, Professor of Child Study at Tufts University and author of *The Hurried Child.* "It is fine for little girls to play with dolls but this one is far removed from what they can understand or appreciate. And what happens if it doesn't work? Is the baby dead?"

As for the crash dummies, Dr. Elkind said: "Children see so much violence on television. Why reinforce it with this kind of toy? Toys should stimulate children's imaginations in positive, not negative ways."

Dr. T. Berry Brazelton, Professor of Pediatrics at Harvard University Medical School, agreed. "I don't like either toy," he said. "The dummies are horrifying to me, and the doll is a real invasion of a parent's opportunity to share something precious with a child. Why do we need such a toy?"

So simple good taste is one very important criterion for toy choice. Another could be violence. Many of the more offensive toys are linked to Saturday morning cartoons that often resemble half-hour commercials for a toy line. Parents who don't watch television with their children are the most susceptible consumers. They may buy warped or violent playthings because they don't understand the significance of the toys, not having seen them in action on television. Peggy Charren, President of Action for Children in Television, says, "the commercial broadcasting industry has given over children's television to the toy companies to produce." She also feels that what children are led to believe the toy does on TV may not actually happen. In 1989 Charren targeted the commercials for several toys as being particularly misleading. Among them were Mattel's Food Fighters; Ring Raiders by Matchbox Toys; Milton Bradley's Guess Who Game; Pogo Ball by Hasbro; Flip Ball by Toy Biz; and Micro Machine Service by Galoob. (Oppenheim, p. 9)

Parents need suggestions on how to deal with false advertising. One way is to take the child to a toy store and show her the actual toy, and then compare it with the advertisement on TV. The child has to be old enough—perhaps five—to comprehend this misrepresentation. Another way is to give the child more quality time and less TV time so the toys on television do not seem so important to own.

Even nonviolent toys seen on and promoted through TV shows have serious drawbacks, according to Diane Levin, Professor of Education at Wheelock College and co-author of the book, *War Play Dilemma*. In an article in *American Health* she observes: "A number of toys on the market are linked to television and are single purpose—they direct children to play in a prescribed way that makes it hard to meet their own developmental needs. As a result, they re-enact scenarios seen on TV or depicted on the toy box" (p. 82). This point is reinforced by Joanne Oppenheim, author of *Buy Me! Buy Me!: The Bank Street Guide to Choosing Toys for Children*, a virtual encyclopedia of toy tips. Oppenheim calls attention to the open-ended nature of today's toy purchase: "Toys are designed virtually to require a multitude of props sold separately—so you're never finished buying. Multiple purchases have replaced multiple uses" (p. 40). So where once a child had an almost limitless number of hoop or yo-yo tricks that involved mastering a complex set of physical and mental skills, there now exists an almost limitless number of outfits for name dolls or components to build a prescribed world for a fantasy character-made-plastic.

So beside the matters of good taste, TV violence and prescribed play, the criterion least open to interpretation is the one that deals with safety. Under the Federal Hazardous Substance Act and the Consumer Safety Act, manufacturing standards have been set by the U.S. Consumer Product Safety Commission (CPSC) for certain toys and children's articles. Toy companies must design and manufacture their products to meet these regulations so that hazardous products are not sold. The Commission has printed a pamphlet—"For Kids Sake—Think Toy Safety," and has listed the nine toy dangers in it:

1. When buying toys, choose toys with care. Keep in mind the child's age, interests, and skill level. Read labels for such as "Not Recommended for Children Under Three." Look for other safety labels including "Flame Retardant"

and "Washable/Hygienic Materials" on stuffed toys and dolls.

2. When maintaining toys check all toys periodically for breakage and potential hazards. A damaged or dangerous toy should be thrown away or repaired immediately.

3. When storing toys teach children to put their toys safely away on shelves or in a toy chest after playing to prevent trips and falls. Also, make sure the toy chest is safe.

4. Sharp edges. New toys intended for children under eight years of age should, by regulation, be free of sharp glass and metal edges.

5. Small parts. Older toys can break to reveal parts small enough to be swallowed or to become lodged in a child's windpipe, ears or nose. The law bans small parts in new toys intended for children under three.

6. Loud noises. Toy cars and some noise-making guns and other toys can produce sounds at noise levels that can damage hearing. The law requires the following label on boxes of caps producing noise above a certain level: "Warning—do not fire closer than one foot to the ear. Do not use indoors."

7. Cords and string. Toys with long strings or cords may be dangerous for infants and very young children. The cords may become wrapped around an infant's neck, causing strangulation.

8. Sharp points. Toys which have been broken may have dangerous points or prongs. A Consumer Products Safety Commission (CPSC) regulation prohibits sharp points in new toys and other articles intended for use by children under eight years of age.

9. Propelled objects. Projectiles, guided missiles and similar flying toys can be turned into weapons and can injure eyes in particular. Children should never be permitted to play with adult lawn darts or other hobby or sporting equipment that has sharp points.

Toys designed for older children should be kept out of the hands of little ones. Older children should be helped to keep their toys away from younger brothers or sisters. Children should be taught to use electric toys properly, cautiously, and under adult supervision.

Although the Consumer Products Safety Commission sets up stringent safety standards that manufacturers are supposed to follow, the Commission cannot enforce these standards because it lacks the funding and personnel to check toys at the manufacturing point. In fact, often the CPSC decides to recall a toy only after a child is injured or dies. The CPSC stated that in 1990 alone, 164,500 children under the age of fifteen suffered toy-related injuries that required treatment in hospital emergency rooms. The Consumer Product Safety Commission reported that thirty-seven children died from toy-related incidents between January 1990 and September 1991. Nineteen of these deaths were the result of choking caused by balloons, marbles, small balls, or toy parts.

The CPSC uses a no-choke testing tube which simulates the size of a young child's throat to determine if small parts of toys can pose a choking hazard to children under the age of three. A testing tube may be ordered for one dollar from:

> Toys to Grow On
> 2695 E. Dominguez St.
> P.O. Box 17
> Long Beach, CA 90801–0017

The CPSC also has a telephone hotline for recall information, complaints about hazardous products and product defects, and for safety pamphlets and fact sheets. The continental United States number is 1–800–638–8326. Thus, it is everybody's responsibility, which includes parents, librarians, and early childhood teachers, to protect children from unsafe toys. Careful toy selection and proper supervision of children at play is still and always will be the best way to protect children from toy-related injuries.

Even if your library does not circulate or use toys, you might want to use the information here as a springboard for starting your own file on toys with an eye to holding parent programs on selecting toys and on toy safety. Such a program would be an invaluable community service and would both help to bring parents into your book program, and would once again enhance the library's standing in the community.

📽 Selected Films and Videos on Play and Toys to Use in Parent Programs

At Your Fingertips: Boxes. Visiting the supermarket, we see a variety of boxes, cartons, and containers which are used in packaging a wide assortment of everyday products. Then at home these same receptacles are transformed into other objects and playthings. 10 minutes. Also video.

Blocks: A Medium for Perception Learning. Focuses on the perceptual learnings that are inherent in block building and are derived from how the child perceives the blocks with which he works and the space in which he builds. The film further details perceptual learning in relation to future academic learning. 17 minutes. Also video.

Dramatic Play. Through live action, dialogue and narration, the film presents the inherent intellectual, social and emotional learning in dramatic play and the strategies used by children in dealing with individuals and materials. The film further details the role of the teacher as an essential part in the total integrating process. Also video.

Foundations of Reading and Writing. Focuses on the learning of reading and writing as an integration of manual skills and basic experiences. Observes children involved in activities with paint, clay, blocks, puzzles, pegs, story reading, music, etc. The film presents some examples of the following: vocabulary with meaning; phonics; word and sentence patterns; rhythmic flow of language; context clues—comprehension, symbol recognition, visual and auditory discrimination, part-whole relationships, configuration, hand-eye coordination, and spatial relationships. 40 minutes.

Hidden in Play. Explores the importance of play in child development, especially for children with disabilities. The film shows children playing at the Lekotek, a play library and counseling center in Evanston, Illinois for children with handicaps and their families.

Let's Play: A New Concept in Parent Education by Roy McConkey. "Let's Play" is a unique course based around six video programs with participant's handbook and tutor's guide. Its aim is to inform parents—mainly of handicapped children under five years of age—how their child learns through play and the ways in which they can help. 130 minutes. Video only.

Outdoor Play. Focuses on the unique opportunities for physical and intellectual development provided by outdoor play activity and presents the extensive use of improved materials. 19 minutes. Also video.

The Tin Toy. This film stars a rambunctious baby and a wind-up music man. The charm of the film lies in the director's ability to infuse inanimate objects with emotions. 5 minutes. Also video.

✂ Some Books About Toys and Play

1. Fisher, John. *More Toys to Grow With.* New York: Putnam, 1987.
2. Fisher, John. *Toys to Grow With.* New York: Putnam, 1986.
3. Garvey, Catherine. *Play.* Cambridge, MA: Harvard University Press, 1977.
4. Gordon, Ira J. *Baby Learning Through Baby Play.* New York: St. Martin's Press, 1970.

5. ———. *Child Learning Through Child Play*. New York: St. Martin's Press, 1972.

6. Kaban, Barbara. *Choosing Toys for Children*. New York: Schocken Books, 1979.

7. Johnson, Doris McNeely. *Children's Toys and Books: Choosing the Best from All Ages from Infancy to Adolescence*. New York: Scribner's, 1982.

8. Marzollo, Jean. *Learning Through Play*. New York: Harper & Row, 1972.

9. Newson, John and Elizabeth. *Toys and Playthings*. New York: Pantheon, 1979.

10. Oppenheim, Joanne. *Buy Me! Buy Me!: The Bank Street Guide to Choosing Toys for Children*. New York: Pantheon, 1987.

11. Parent-Child Early Education Program. *Games to Grow On: The First Year*. Ferguson, MO.: Ferguson-Florissant, 1976.

12. Piers, Maria W. *The Gift of Play and Why Young Children Cannot Thrive Without It*. New York: Walker, 1980.

13. Singer, Dorothy G. and Jerome L. *The House of Make-Believe: Children's Play and the Developing Imagination*. Cambridge, MA.: Harvard University Press, 1990.

14. Sinker, Mary. *Toys for Growing: A Guide to Toys That Develop Skills*. Chicago: Year Book Medical Publishers, 1986.

15. Swartz, Edward. *Toys That Don't Care*. Boston: Gambit, 1971.

16. Sutton-Smith, Brian and Shirley. *How to Play with Your Child and When Not To*. New York: Hawthorn, 1974.

17. Wiseman, Ann. *Making Musical Things*. New York: Scribner's, 1979.

Resources to Help Organize a Toy Library

1. American Library Association. *Toys to Go: A Guide to the Use of Realia in Public Libraries*. Chicago: ALA, 1975. First published by means of a LSCA grant from the Connecticut State Library.

2. Far West Laboratory for Educational Research and Development. *The Parent/Child Toy Lending Library*. Superintendent of Documents, Washington, D.C.: U.S. Government Printing Office, 1972.
3. Canadian Association of Toy Libraries. *Toy Libraries—How to Start a Toy Library in Your Community*. Toronto: CATL, 1978.
4. Canadian Association of Toy Libraries. *Toy Libraries 2— The Many Uses of Toy Lending*. Toronto: CATL, 1980.
5. Sinker, Mary. *The Lekotek Guide to Good Toys*. Evanston, IL: North Shore Lekotek, 1983.

7

Influencing At-Home Reading and Organizing a TV Turn-Off

The real point of programming for preschoolers is twofold: to stimulate the children's interest in books and reading, and to stimulate parents and other caregivers to nurture it well. The children's librarian who runs parent-child programs is therefore in a unique position to subtly (and often not-so-subtly) influence what reading and book-related activities go on in the home. Songs, rhymes, storytelling, fingerplays, games, and interactive generational play are all possible facets that parents can pick up on. In our fragmented society, where the nuclear family is often cut off from itself through divorce or separation, and from the older generation of grandparents and the traditions they can foster, the children's librarian can serve as the model for such involvement activities.

"Give a man a fish and you feed him once. Teach him to fish and you feed him for life." This bit of folk wisdom sums up the librarian's role: in and of themselves the programs only sustain while they sustain. If you teach the parents, however, the programming can continue at any time. This is why programs must be set up in such a way as to accommodate the needs of parents as well as children. It may be tempting, for instance, to sign up lots of people, but overcrowding can defeat your purpose: keeping your groups small, you can talk to all the children and parents individually, to explain, highlight, praise, and consult as a way of building confidence and understanding. You'd be surprised at how this "personal touch" will work for you and even (as in some of my programs) earn you a round of applause.

Some participation story hours should be scheduled for the evening. This often enables working mothers or fathers to come, or the parent who works the day shift outside the home. If the night-time story hours do not involve the parent directly, at least parents are brought to the library and will have the chance to choose materials to use at home with their child.

At best, parents are the child's first and most important teachers and have the greatest influence during the first crucial five years of life. Ideally, the parent should be a good role model, in reading as in other aspects of parenting. It has been found that children who begin to read successfully usually enjoy three clear advantages over nonreading children:

1. A parent or caregiver who reads to the child.

2. A parent of caregiver who regularly reads *in front of the child*.

3. Plenty of books and magazines in the home, easily accessible.

There are several early goals for parents that you can support in the library program. The first of these is to promote the self esteem of the child. Parents can do this by making the child feel good, and competent—as someone who can do something. If a child feels unliked, or is made to feel incompetent, he may become aggressive or withdrawn. Children need to be liked in order to feel successful.

A second goal for parents is to help the child make good decisions. Showing them cause and effect relationships—that behavior has its consequences and that actions do not happen in a vacuum, but in fact lead to other actions which involve other people, is the beginning of the sense of responsibility. If, for instance, you are reading *Where's Spot?* to your toddler group (and parents), you can pause and have the children try to think before they open the flaps to find Spot. It doesn't matter, of course, whether the child is right or wrong, but that the child tried to go through a thought process before "finding" the answer.

A third goal is to help parents understand what is age-appropriate behavior. A good example I see every day is "sharing." Helping the child share can be tiring, frustrating, rewarding, exasperating, and even anger-provoking for parent as well as child. In our programs for parents and children under three years of age, we make available different kinds of materials at the end of the program for the children. We use toys or puppets or musical instruments, and make sure there are enough to go around. However, the children do not share and tend to grab things from each other. It is very hard for parents to deal with this behavior and they try to explain to their children about sharing, or to discipline them. At this point I give them an excellent handout from the Children's Museum of Boston titled "Helping Your Child Share."

This handout states that parents can't hasten the tendency to share. There are some excellent quotes about sharing from several childcare books including Dr. Benjamin Spock's *Baby and Child Care*, Selma H. Fraiberg's *The Magic Years*, and Robbie Harris and Elizabeth Levy's *Before You Were Three*. In the sharing concept the definition of identity is important and nowhere is it better explained than in L. Joseph Stone's *Childhood and Adolescence*:

> Many toddlers are vividly aware of ownership, may spend a large amount of time labeling objects with the names of their owners, and fiercely resist use of any object by someone who is not its owner. Such possessiveness may apply to other people's belongings before the toddler begins to defend his own against encroachment. Many parents with an altruistic bent try to bring up their children in a spirit of openhanded sharing, and are disappointed when a toddler seems to be selfish about his own possessions. It seems to be the case that almost all toddlers and young preschool children go through a period of possessiveness, which may be an important step in

the definition of an identity and the articulation of relationships in the outside world, and which cannot be rushed. (p. 241–42)

One good way to get parents to bring your programming ideas home is to give them a list. Charlotte J. Sharpe, a former reading consultant to the Farmington, Connecticut schools, prepared a handout for us called "Activities Related to Reading Readiness." She divides readiness activities into seven parts that parents can easily try to incorporate into their daily routines.

Activities Related to Reading Readiness

I.   Physical Activities

1. LARGE MUSCLE GROUPS
Skipping
Hopping
Galloping
Tiptoeing
Walking
Jumping
Somersaults
Walking a plank

Keeping a balloon in the air
Rolling a ball
Bouncing a ball
Catching a ball (use a large ball and gradually over the years decrease the size)

2. SMALL MUSCLE GROUPS
Fingerplays, puppets
Squeezing clay
Lacing
Buttoning
Stringing beads, macaroni, etc.
Braiding

Squeezing a rubber ball
Pouring (pour uncooked rice from one cup to another)
Sweeping (with a child-size broom)
Dressing oneself
Zipping zippers

II.   Left-to-Right Progression

1. When reading a story to your child occasionally point to words as you read.

2. Put pictures that tell a story in sequence from left to right.

3. Play games like "Looby Loo" or "Simon Says."

4. Talk about *left* and *right*. Give simple directions at home using these words.

5. Talk about pictures of people, animals, etc., facing different directions.

III. Environmental Concepts

1. Talk with your child about what he sees and hears

- Weather and seasons
- Sounds: loud-soft; louder-softer; etc.
- Kinds of animals and their uses
- Kinds of clothing and their uses
- Kinds of groceries and their uses
- Your family and others; their experiences
- Sizes: tall-short; big-little; large-small; etc.

2. If trips away from home are taken, discuss what is seen and experienced.

IV. Color Concepts

1. Talk about and identify color of clothes, toys, household items, groceries, etc.

2. Match colors using paper, buttons, fabric, etc.

3. Talk about lighter and darker shades of primary colors.

V. Visual Discrimination

1. To explore likenesses and differences, compare:
   - Sizes
   - Textures
   - Shapes
   - Colors

2. We use many books in the toddler to three-year-old programs that are concerned with visual discrimination. Some of our most popular ones are:

- *Where's the Fish?* by Taro Gomi. You have to find the small pink fish that leaps straight out of his fish bowl and plays a colorful game of hide-and-seek.
- *It's Mine* by Rod Campbell. Let's take a walk in the tall grass by the river. We might see some animals— are you ready? A part of the animal is shown and the child has to guess what animal it is.
- *Each Peach Pear Plum* by Janet and Allan Ahlberg. Very young children can spy familiar nursery charac- ters hiding in the delightful pictures.
- *Tail, Toes, Eyes, Ears, Nose* by Marilee R. Burton. Here is a delightful guessing game that highlights eight familiar animals.
- *Guess Who?* by Pam Ayres. "Piglets jumping off a bale/ Who has lost his curly tail?" The child has to pick out the one pig that has a straight tail and so on through the book.
- *I Spy at the Zoo* by Maureen Roffey. Children have fun spotting favorite animals and the busy people that fill the pages of this book.
- *Which Witch is Which?* by Pat Hutchins. Ella and Emily go to a fancy dress party as witches. These identical twins wear identical costumes but clues are provided.
- *Where Is Clifford?* by Norman Bridwell. We are looking for our favorite big red dog in a lift-a-flap book.
- *Sebastian* by Vanessa Julian-Ottie. Children will delight in following Sebastian the curious kitten, and see what he sees.

3. Puzzles. Begin with three and four pieces and advance. Start with these:

- Ice Cream Cone Puzzle (Salco). A wooden two-piece puzzle.

- Three Piece Puzzle, Board and Shapes (Salco). A knobbed wooden puzzle.
- Four Ducks (Childcraft). A wooden knob puzzle.
- Four Wood Puzzles (Didago). Four shape puzzles. Each puzzle has five pieces.
- Kid's Puzzle (Lauri). A foam rubber puzzle. Children must pay close attention to small detail and slight variations to make each piece fit into its correct space.

(The uses and importance of puzzles are discussed in the film *Foundations of Reading and Writing*).

VI. Listening

1. Tell stories, discuss things with your child, talk about events in the order of their occurrence.
2. Give very brief instructions to be completed by the child.
3. Listen to sounds around you and distinguish them with the child.
4. Play a wide variety of records or tapes or compact discs. Auditory discrimination is important to teach children. Here is a sample of some listening records and songs that are especially pertinent.

   - *Music for 1's and 2's* by Tom Glazer. Song: "Big and Little." The child listens to big sounds and little sounds, such as a lion's roar and a little kitten's meow.
   - *Songs About Me, Volume III* by William Janiak. Song: "If You Have This On Stand Up, Sit Down." This record combines the concepts of standing up and sitting down with clapping, slapping knees and stamping feet, as well as listening and making the right vowel sounds.
   - *Learning Basic Skills Through Music, Volume I* by Hap Palmer. Song: "Colors." Give the children different colored papers and have them stand up or sit down when their color is called.

VII. Reading

1. Read often—daily if possible—to your child.

2. Let your child "read" pictures to you.

3. Use a wordless book to have the child tell you the story (three-year-olds love this). Record the story on tape and play it back for your child. These are some of the fine wordless books that are adaptable to this activity:

   - *The Adventures of Paddy Pork* by John Goodall
   - *A Boy, a Dog, and a Frog* by Mercer Mayer
   - *Sunlight* by Jan Ormerod
   - *The Bear and the Fly* by Paula Winter
   - *Deep in the Forest* by Brinton Turkle

4. Use picture books for reading and telling stories.

5. Read labels on grocery items, etc.

6. Be a regular reader yourself.

7. Use your public library.

For more parental reading encouragement you could send for a free pamphlet from the Barbara Bush Foundation for Family Literacy, 1002 Wisconsin Avenue, N.W., Washington, D.C. 20007. It is titled *Barbara Bush's Family Reading Tips.*

She lists nine tips for reading aloud and more information under each suggestion. The following is a bare outline from her pamphlet.

1. Establish a routine for reading aloud.

2. Make reading together a special time.

3. Try these simple ways to enrich your reading aloud: Move your finger under the words as you read. (There are six more suggestions under this tip.)

4. Ask others who take care of your children to read aloud.

5. Visit the library regularly.

6. Let your children see you reading.

7. Read all kinds of things together.
8. Fill your home with opportunities for reading.
9. Keep reading aloud even after your children learn to read.

Certainly the best-known champion of reading aloud is Jim Trelease, who packs a great deal of practical information and reading research into *The New Read-Aloud Handbook*. His list of "The Do's and Don'ts of Read-Aloud" can be suggested to parents, along with his book lists—there is even one for wordless books. Most recently Trelease has created an anthology of stories that older children, from kindergarten to fourth grade, will love, called *Hey! Listen to This: Stories to Read Aloud*. Audiocassettes and 16mm films of Trelease's popular lectures can be ordered from Reading Tree Productions, 51 Arvesta St., Springfield, MA 01118.

REASONS PRESCHOOL CHILDREN BECOME ATTACHED TO BOOKS

In our programs parents are always asking why children become attached to certain books, or why one book appeals more than another. Often they can see no rhyme or reason for a child's choice, but I can usually tell them why. There are nine reasons that could fit the case, and once you know them, and know the child, it's not difficult to see why some books achieve favored status. In many cases the reasons can overlap, but here they are, complete with book examples that will help you in your own programs.

1. It meets the need for reassurance. *Sam Who Never Forgets* by Eve Rice meets the need that children have to be taken care of and not forgotten. The child will see the elephant as himself and will see Sam, the zookeeper, as the parent who is taking care of him.
   Where the Wild Things Are by Maurice Sendak fills another need. The child always wants to be boss, and in

this story Max becomes King of the Wild Things. Although the monsters in the book are very popular with young children, it is Max, in command of his world, who strongly appeals to them.

Whose Mouse Are You? by Robert Kraus is a book I use with all children, but it is especially good to use with emotionally disturbed children because it is so satisfying. There are great family relationships in the book. The picture of the father mouse and his son racing around the cheeses in their sports cars is one of the best illustrations of a father-son relationship that there is in children's books.

2. The child can identify with it. Through identifying with the characters, the child sees the book as an extension of himself. All the *Sam* books by Barbro Lindgren can qualify: *Sam's Ball, Sam's Bath, Sam's Car, Sam's Cookie, Sam's Lamp, Sam's Potty, Sam's Teddy Bear,* and *Sam's Wagon.* Sam is a typical toddler who has all kinds of typical toddler problems and children relate very easily to this delightful child.

The Wild Baby by Barbro Lindgren is for an older child and there are three in the *Wild Baby* series. The other two are *The Wild Baby Goes to Sea* and *The Wild Baby Gets a Puppy.* Ben, the wild baby, has many escapades testing the strength of his mother's love. Children love these books more than their parents, who will question if Sam or Ben is going to lead their child into trouble. The child, of course, knows that she can think up all these activities on her own.

3. It's a funny book. Children love to laugh and love books that are humorous. They will want to hear them over and over again. All the original H. A. Rey *Curious George* books are high on their list, along with the *Harry the Dirty Dog* series by Gene Zion.

4. The book is predictable or repetitious. Children like to be able to "read" to themselves, so even two-year-olds will

memorize books. Two of our books most in demand for two-year-olds are *Brown Bear, Brown Bear, What Do You See?* by Bill Martin, Jr., and *A Dark Dark Tale* by Ruth Brown. The latter always amazes me but it is a favorite because of the repetition and the predictable end. Two of the favorite books for three-year-olds are *The Three Billy Goats Gruff* by Paul Galdone and *The Old Woman and Her Pig* by Paul Galdone. As the children soon learn these books by heart, they do not want any words left out when they are read to them.

5. The book is an arty book, or just different from the others. My daughter, Sally, was given two books for Christmas when she was a year and a half. One was *Goodnight Moon* by Margaret Wise Brown, which she liked, and the other was *Zoo* by Bruno Munari, which she absolutely adored and had to have read several times a day. This is not a book that appeals to many young children and ninety-nine out of one hundred would prefer *Goodnight Moon*. But this book seemed different to her, probably because of the unusual artwork. *Frederick* by Leo Lionni is a beautiful book too, and a Caldecott Honor Award winner, but I have not found many children through the years as crazy about this book as Sally was. Parents and librarians should expose children to many different kinds of books so the child can pick out his or her favorite.

6. The book has rhythm. Children love rhythm books and one of their favorites is *Hand, Hand, Finger, Thumb* by Al Perkins. This book is on our "I Can Read" shelf but because of the wonderful rhythm, I use it in my toddler groups and on up. A second book which is already a favorite is the rollicking rhyming book *Sheep in a Jeep* by Nancy Shaw. The illustrations are also delightful. Of the two follow-up books, *Sheep on a Ship* and *Sheep in a Shop*, the latter is as wonderful as *Sheep in a Jeep*.

7. There is a happy event associated with the book. Many children love the book *Make Way for Ducklings* by Robert

McCloskey, because they have been to the public gardens in Boston where the mallards took their ducklings. From then on when the book is read, they remember their happy experience. Another book in this category could be *The Circus Baby* by Maud and Miska Petersham. After going to the circus, children may want to hear this book again and again.

8. The book is a gimmick, toy, or game. Children love peek-a-boo books, for instance, because it is their favorite game. Two such favorites are *Dear Zoo* by Rod Campbell and *Where's Spot?* by Eric Hill. We always encourage parents to buy these books as the library copies can get dilapidated pretty quickly and children always want the flaps to be intact. Another well-loved book is *What's for Lunch?* by Eric Carle. The children are fascinated by the monkey who slides on a string to find his favorite fruit.

9. A child has real interest in the subject. Children develop early a fascination for trucks, fire engines, trains, and other large machines. *Freight Train* by Donald Crews is one such book that provides this experience. I use *Big Wheels* by Anne Rockwell in my Toddler II group and am always amazed that several of the toddlers can give me the names of all the big-wheeled vehicles in the book. A great nonfiction series for children two and up are the Eye Openers books. These include *Farm Animals* by Philip Dowell, *Zoo Animals* by Philip Dowell, *Jungle Animals* by Angela Royston, and *Diggers and Dump Trucks* by Angela Royston.

WATER PLAY

An activity that we don't do in the library but really encourage parents to do at home is water play. Playing in the water is very relaxing for young children, and fascinating for older children as well. All ages like being able to manipulate, to mess around, and to see the results of their efforts—well worth a few soggy towels. The young child can play in the kitchen or bathroom sink or tub where she can pour and dump to her heart's content. All children must be supervised, of course, and watched very carefully by a responsible adult. Warn parents of the dangers of water, of chairs that fall over, slippery floors, and nearby electricity—all occupational hazards. Many nursery schools and day care centers have water play tables to encourage water play activity.

These are some of the more popular water toys to recommend to parents.

- Bathtime Friends (Hand in Hand). A set of play stickers that magically cling like wet cloths to tub, shower and pool surface. They also will float.
- Froggie's Fleet (Discovery). Froggie has four plastic water-tight boats that fit in each other or can float separately.
- Water Activity Playset (Battat). This bathtub activity center sticks to the tub wall with suction cups. Activities include a man that hides and seeks in the tower, an octopus who squirts water, a water wheel that spins and a trough at the top to fill with water which starts all other activities.
- Boat Activity Puzzle (Battat). Geometrically-shaped activity blocks fit snugly into bottom of sturdy boat. Action blocks include waterwheel, whistle, a squirting pump, and a pop-up man.
- Floating Fish (Battat). Three colorful fish all float, and all link together.
- Water Activity (Ambi). This is a companion piece to Active Baby. (See chapter 6, p. 102) There is a squirter, a water wheel and a little watering can.
- Ball in a Bowl (Johnson & Johnson). There are three little plastic balls that fit into a larger plastic bowl. This toy can be used in the tub or out but children much prefer the toy as a water activity.
- Play Buckets (Kiddicraft). There are three buckets: one has

a spout, another has a hole where the mouth should be, and the third has a sieve bottom.

- Mother Duck (Kiddicraft). Mother duck has three small ducklings that can be loaded on her back.
- Giant Building Beakers (Gowi). There are seven beakers that the child can use for pouring water or for stacking.
- Noah's Ark Toy Set (Tuppertoys). A plastic boat that includes six animals, a ramp and two people.
- Flippy Duck (Battat). Bright yellow duck has strong suction cup to attach to the bathtub. Use his hat to pour water into duck. Beak, wings, and feet flap as water flows through.
- Sand-Water Mill (Bambola). With this toy the child can channel sand or water and start and stop the flow and in the process begin to understand the basic mechanics of the funnel, slideway door, and waterwheel.
- Handy Boxes (Ambi). There are six nesting boxes which can be used in both sand and water play as scoops and containers.
- Water Play Pump (Galt). Kids just pump the handle to watch water fill the plastic tube, then splash out the spout.
- Watering Can (Galt). Kids love to fill this small watering can and dump it out, only to fill it again and dump it out, etc.
- Tub Pals (Playskool). This toy comes with three little sailors that float in and out of their little boats.
- Wind-up Sea Plane (Playskool). This boat-plane is easy for young children to operate in the bathtub.
- Stacking Sand and Water Wheel (Childcraft). The children use the scoop to pour sand or water through the small top funnel, and then watch it cascade into the wheels to make them turn, then drop down to spin the next set of wheels.
- Water Scoops (Battat). Three different primary-colored scoops and a floating ball invite waterplay fun. Plain scoop, pouring scoop and sieve scoop also fit inside each other.
- Water Wheel (Galt). This toy has a suction cup that

adheres to the bathtub. There is a storage trough at the top that the child fills with water. As the water trickles through, the water wheel revolves.

THE INFLUENCE OF TELEVISION

Going back to the three factors in home life that children who begin to read enjoy, we can see that number two is *a parent or caregiver who regularly reads in front of the child.* What was not said is that parents who are television-watchers primarily, *not* readers, influence the child indirectly *away* from books and reading. The TV is supreme in many homes: often there is more than one—sometimes even three or four of these one-eyed monsters—and family members may have their own TVs. Often the set is left on all the time, when no one is watching, or even when no one is in the room. The message clearly given to the young child is this: THE TELEVISION IS IMPORTANT.

Much has been written about television and children and although there are creative uses of television, there is much abuse—especially when it takes the young child away from play. As Piers and Landau, experts in child development and psychology, state in the book, *The Gift of Play:*

> Young children today are even further cut off from the real world—and from their inner selves—by a pervasive intruder in their lives that smothers their opportunities to learn through play. This intruder is television. Today, children between the ages of two and five comprise the largest television audience in the United States. In home after home, preschoolers spend over thirty hours a week glued to the TV set. A substantial number watch up to sixty hours of TV a week. To put that figure in full perspective, this means that in many instances virtually all the young child's waking hours are spent watching television. Steady exposure to the bombardment of TV images stunts the emotional and mental development of children. Heavy TV viewing can actually retard the development of the child's whole personality and character with far-reaching and perilous consequences to the children involved and to society as a whole.
>
> The early childhood years are, indeed, the crucial years for development. Just as a tree can be dwarfed and twisted in its early years of growth, so can

a person's eventual "configuration" be misshaped if normal early patterns of development are seriously interfered with. And a heavy TV diet in the pre-school years does just that. It impedes children's normal development since there is no chance to respond actively, creatively to the stimuli imposed on them, little opportunity to exercise their imaginations, think their own thoughts, play with their own games. (p. 17–18)

TURNING OFF THE TV

As much as we would sometimes like to, we cannot sneak into people's homes and turn off their TV sets so they will read, and will read to their children. What we *can* do is to touch each family in our community through a community-wide effort to curb television watching. It's been done, and done successfully.

The Great TV Turn-Off happened in Farmington in January of 1984, and each year for four years thereafter, with the enthusiastic nurturance of participants, educators, and the media. The idea for a TV Turn-Off month came into being in the public library under the sponsorship of the Farmington Library Council during my presidency. The council consisted of librarians from each public school library and public library, a representative from the public schools, librarians from area private schools and universities, and the owner of a local bookstore. We were all greatly influenced in our desire to run a TV Turn-Off by two well-known people who had come as speakers to our group. One was Marie Winn, author of *The Plug-In Drug*, and the other was Jim Trelease, whose *Read-Aloud Handbook*, which has since influenced so many parents, was just being published.

Our starting point was the simple growing concern that children were spending too much leisure time watching television. By encouraging families to turn the TV off for a month, we hoped that people would "turn on" to reading, or spend more time working at hobbies, playing games, talking with one another, and doing more physical activities. Preschoolers, we hoped, would spend more time in imaginative play.

To begin with, we never advocated turning off television

forever, but instead urged members of the community to follow guidelines for watching, especially with preschoolers. These were based on the work of Dorothy G. and Jerome L. Singer, psychologists who have worked extensively with parents through Yale University's Family Television Research and Consultation Center. Dorothy G. Singer is the William Benton Professor of Psychology at the University of Bridgeport, Connecticut, and Jerome L. Singer is Professor of Psychology and Child Study and Director of Graduate Studies in Psychology at Yale University. Among their suggestions for parents given at a lecture at the Farmington Library were:

1. Limit TV viewing to one hour per day for preschoolers.

2. Avoid programs with excessive spookiness, unexplained supernatural figures, direct violence or physical attacks.

3. Select cartoons carefully; discuss what is real and what is fantasy.

4. Watch TV with your child, including the news and other adult specials.

5. Provide explanation and balanced information about stereotypes.

6. Be careful of extremely risky athletic tricks; kids may try to imitate them.

7. Try to use ideas from TV for more active play/learning with your child.

‍ Running a TV Turn-Off

As a result of the very successful and well publicized Farmington TV Turn-Off in 1984, we were besieged by other agencies to explain how we accomplished it. The Farmington Library Council's TV Turn-Off Kit was developed to help other communities, schools, or libraries to develop their own approach to reducing the television viewing of adults and, particularly, children. The Farmington TV Turn-Off experience involved educational leaders in the process early on and its success resulted from having key persons in each school (librarians and school administrators) and the entire staff of the public library actively supporting the Turn-Off and promoting its goals. The kit has many ideas and suggestions for making your efforts successful. These include:

1. Planning your TV Turn-Off. The fourteen points from this section are enumerated here below.

2. What to do during the Turn-Off: lists of activities.

3. Letter from Farmington educators and parents on the effects of the Turn-Off.

4. Farmington TV Turn-Off: a review of the Farmington experience, January 1984.

5. Evaluation of the Farmington experience.

6. Television Viewing and Children - A review of selected research.

7. Bibliographies.

This kit can be ordered from The Farmington Library, 6 Monteith Drive, Farmington, CT 06032 for $7.50. The check can be made out to the Farmington Library.

As a result of what we learned we have been able to help other communities and, in one spectacular instance, an entire nation! From June 21–27, 1992, New Zealand held its own country-wide TV Turn-Off, producing its own kit, which was mailed to 2,800 public schools and scores of preschools. Results of the Turn-Off are not yet tabulated, but copies of the handbook may be obtained from the New Zealand Public Library Association, Box 12–212, Wellington, New Zealand at a small cost. The contents of this handbook may also be reproduced if credit is given.

📖 Fourteen Points for Planning Your TV Turn-Off from the Farmington Library

1. Schedule a meeting of school and public librarians. Invite others who you feel would be interested, such as a reading

consultant, school administrator, board of education member and/or town council representative and a representative from a civic or service organization. You will need a good base support group to get your program off the ground at all levels. Coordinating a program through both the schools and the public library enables you to reach all age groups. Be sure to leave yourself plenty of planning time. In some communities a civic or social agency may be willing to co-sponsor the Turn-Off.

2. Draw up a resolution to bring to your Board of Education to gain support for the program. (An example of a resolution is provided in the kit).

3. Design your "cold turkey cards" and bumper stickers or whatever you decide to use as a promotion. Remember to print enough cards so that they may be distributed to each student in the school system and be available at the public library and the other community centers for preschoolers and adults. These cards will be used for documenting participation in the project and for evaluating the effectiveness of your Turn-Off. (Examples are provided in the kit).

4. Plan an opening night "kick-off" program in the town. We held a forum with speakers, including a local TV anchorwoman, the superintendent of schools, a board of education member, a teacher, a parent, and a high school student. (Sample announcement provided in the kit).

5. If possible, hold teacher workshops to promote the program and suggest activities for classrooms. Have available a reading list for professionals (see bibliography in the kit) and, if possible, student reading lists so that teacher may help their students select reading materials as a TV alternative.

6. Plan activities to maintain interest in the Turn-Off at the schools and at the public libraries. There is an "Activity" section in the kit with suggestions. Contact your local recreation centers to inform them of the program. People

will have more free time and will be looking for activities. (Examples of public library publicity are included in the kit).

7. Make plans for some sort of townwide activities in which anyone can participate. As an example, Farmington held a student writing contest. An awards ceremony for this contest provided a great way to end the Turn-Off. Details on planning this contest are included in the "Activity" section of the packet. (Contest rules and publicity are provided in the kit).

8. Write a letter explaining the program to parents and arrange for it to be distributed in the schools just prior to the beginning of the program.

9. Write a news release to explain the program. Be sure to include the reasons why you are suggesting the Turn-Off and highlight the activities to be offered throughout the program. You may want to include a copy of the resolution passed by your board of education or town council. (Examples in kit).

10. Contact the newspapers and plan to have a weekly list printed of activities being offered at the public library. Remember that people will have more free time on their hands and they will want to know what they can do as an alternative to watching TV. Libraries can expect an increase in circulation and also in program attendance. This will be a good chance to reach prospective patrons.

11. If you are planning a contest or other activities requiring prizes, begin to write letters to community service organizations for donations. Don't forget to try local businesses. They may also help out.

12. Let the program begin! Whether you hear people talking positively or negatively about the program, they at least will be talking about it! This accomplishes part of your goal, which is to make people aware of the TV they now watch. Hint: If you find yourself with a deluge of media

interviews, you may want to keep an information sheet near the telephone with such statistics as town population, school population, etc. Also, prepare a list of a few families prior to the Turn-Off who will participate in the program and who would not mind being interviewed. We found that TV crews especially liked to visit the schools and then "go home" with a family. Also, prepare a list of families *not* participating who would be willing to talk with the media.

13. Statistics can be very interesting! Conduct a survey concerning the program. Classes at the schools can be asked to participate in the survey; public library patrons can fill out survey forms, too. A copy of the survey used at Farmington's junior high is included in the kit.

14. Plan follow-up activities which deal with the use of leisure time and how to become more discriminating in TV viewing. People will be more aware of the time spent in front of the TV and it is a good chance to stress an evaluation of that time.

RESPONSES TO THE FARMINGTON
TV TURN-OFF

Once the TV Turn-Off has taken place in your community, you'll be able to measure your success by the letters and comments you receive and from letters to the local papers. (You can even get permission from correspondents to use their comments in the paper, generating further publicity for the library). The comments we received were gratifying and enlightening. The benefits of turning off the tube, it seems, were greater, and more far-reaching, than we would have predicted. Here are some of the results.

Less fatigue, less violence

From a kindergarten teacher—

"During January, when Farmington turned off TV, I didn't

notice a big difference in individual children. However, I did notice a difference in the *class*. The children were less tired, their play was less violent, and they were better listeners. The children talked about many activities they had participated in with their families. Many more books were brought in for us to read because they were 'good books Mom and Dad had read.' The kindergarten children seem to have been watching a great deal of TV before January. One of their favorite programs was 'The A-Team.' It was not uncommon for one-third to one-half of the class to have been up until 9:00 p.m. the evening before watching TV. This certainly had an effect on learning and school behavior.

"I think that no-TV month was great. Hopefully parents and children will be more selective about TV watching. They may now use TV to their advantage instead of letting it dictate their activities (or lack of activity!). At least now we all are aware of the role TV plays in our lives.

"I am very concerned with the number of hours children sit in front of the TV. They do not have to be kind, considerate, understanding, with a TV. They are not having any interaction with other people. We need to develop these 'human *skills*.' "

✄ Sensitivity to others

From a preschool teacher—
"Over the last ten years, I've seen a change in children's imaginative play. The traditional doctor, nurse, police, fireman, family role-playing has been replaced with TV movie heroes such as Luke Skywalker, Princess Leia, Mr. 'T' and so on. Imitative play has taken over imaginative play in role-playing situations. Often loud, aggressive, physical behavior accompanies 'super hero' play. Even the child who does not view these TV shows gets caught up in this play. The few that are so easily stimulated are often frequent TV viewers. The TV will hold these otherwise very active children's attention.

"My greatest concern the last few years is the apparent insensitivity more and more children have when it comes to their peers' feelings and physical well-being. They get caught up in this 'macho' play and become physically careless about their peers.

"Parents must be made aware of some of the negative effects TV has on their young child. It is up to us as parents, teachers, caregivers and community leaders to provide positive experiences allowing the young child to develop to his optimum. That means intellectually, socially, and physically."

More independence, more resourcefulness

From a parent—
"Our family turned off our television for the month of January as part of the 'Farmington TV Turn-Off' project. We did not find it to be a hardship, but rather an interesting learning experience which has provided us with lasting benefits. Although prior to January we were not heavy TV watchers, we all had our own levels of 'dependence' on the TV and we all anxiously antici-pated how we would cope with the absence of television.

"The main component which made this a successful project in our household was the support and encouragement from the schools and the library. Our seven-year-old son eagerly partici-pated because it was a 'fun' community project and an exciting challenge to see if he could do it! Prior to January he did not spend much time watching television anyway, so this did not present a major change for him. His busy daily schedule left him no time for TV on school nights. Whenever possible, however, he would watch cartoons for a limited amount of time on weekend mornings. During the Turn-Off it was amazing to see the number of things he could find to keep himself occupied on Saturday mornings.

"We had anticipated more difficulty with our three-year-old daughter. Being ill recently, she had discovered that in addition to 'Sesame Street' and 'Mr. Rogers' there were children's shows on our cable channels almost any hour of the day. While we did not object to the subject matter of many of these shows, my husband and I were concerned with the fact that she was being passively entertained for two to three hours a day. It had become increasingly difficult to distract her away from it. We took advantage of this Turn-Off campaign to 'wean' her from the TV. We expected resistance. We did not expect the results to be so successful or so easy. Anticipating at the very least an argument, we casually mentioned to her the approaching Turn-Off, stressing that the library (one of her favorite spots) and schools had suggested it. To our surprise, her response was a cheery, 'OK!' To her, the fact that the library had suggested the idea made it acceptable, even fun. My husband and I both know full well that if we had suggested it as our own idea it would have caused a lot of arguments, may have been viewed as punishment, and in the end probably would not have worked.

"For the first week or so of the Turn-Off she mentioned her favorite shows every once in awhile and said that she missed them. After that she didn't seem to give them a thought. At first I had to be sure to have activities ready to keep her occupied, especially at critical times like when I was preparing dinner. I soon found that she was able to think of things to do to entertain herself without my guidance. In my opinion this development of independent resourcefulness is one of the major advantages of shutting off the TV. Children find they don't have to sit passively and be entertained. Instead, they can actively make their own fun!

"What is most thrilling to use about this whole project is the fact that now, some three months later, the effect of it is still with us! While my husband and I have tended to fall back on our old ways, the lasting effect on our children has been overwhelming! Not only do our children *not* watch TV now—except for special events—they don't even think about it! In the last three months they have only watched a handful of selected shows such as some Olympic coverage, space shuttle launchings, and *The Wizard of Oz*. They now, especially the three-year-old, spend their time more creatively and actively. They have kicked the habit!"

🎛 More family pride

From a parent—

"There are of course two sides to every issue: the TV Turn-Off one is no exception. I could write reasons for both.

"Instead, my mind keeps coming back to, and I keep focusing on, the most apparent result of becoming a family committed to Farmington's TV Turn-Off—the pride we all gained in being committed, of surviving (and even enjoying!) doing without, of stretching ourselves in the pursuit of trying something new (and I guess daring!). Like any discipline that we endeavor to follow, if we are successful (and we were—in so many ways!), we grow, we learn about ourselves, we take pleasure in the fact that we have done well.

"As a family we are proud of ourselves and of each other for having made this effort together—and for doing so well. *Nothing* we could have watched all month would have given us that."

🎛 *In Conclusion* _____

No book can cover the many ways that a children's librarian may influence the future lives of youngsters. We can only offer suggestions, and only keep trying to reach out into the community toward parents, teachers, daycare people, other caregivers, and of course the children themselves, and bring to them what we know best: books, other media, and the wonderful objects of childhood — toys. We know what powerful tools we hold. We know the look in a child's face when just the right book speaks to him or to her. And *we* know how pleased adults can be with just simple things—new to them perhaps, and so familiar to us— that bring light into their child's life. The more we can learn the better we can teach, for we are teachers—subtle ones, perhaps, but teachers nonetheless. So it behooves us to find out more about these children who come into our library, and to understand how they differ from stage to stage of their young lives. Then we really will be able to address their needs, and help them get started on the road to books and reading.

Appendix 1

New Baby Books

Here are selected titles to recommend for reading to young siblings of an expected or newborn baby.

Arthur's Baby. Marc T. Brown
Baby Blanket Blues. Angela Terry
A Baby Sister for Frances. Russell Hoban
Ben's Baby. Michael Foreman
Betsy's Baby Brother. Gunilla Wolde
Big Sisters Are Bad Witches. Morse Hamilton
Billy and Our New Baby. Helene S. Arnstein
Changes. Anthony Browne
Chuckie. Nicki Weiss
Everett Anderson's Nine Month Long. Lucille Clifton
Greenbrook Farm. Bonnie Pryor
How You Were Born. Joanna Cole
It's a Baby! George Ancona
I Want a Brother or Sister. Astrid Lindgren
Jenny's Baby Brother. Peter Smith
Jenny's New Baby Sister. Bonnie Pryor
Jeremy Isn't Hungry. Barbara Williams
Katie Did! Kathryn Galbraith

Katie Morag and the Tiresome Ted. Mairi Hedderwich
Let Me Tell You About My Baby. Roslyn Banish
Me Baby! Riki Levinson
The Monster in the Third Dresser Drawer. Janice Lee Smith
My Baby Brother Needs a Friend. Jane B. Moncure
My Brother Will. Joan Robins
My Name Is Emily. Morse and Emily Hamilton
The New Baby. Mercer Mayer
New Baby. Emily Arnold McCully
The New Baby. Fred Rogers
The New Baby. Cyndy Szekeres
The New Baby at Your House. Joanna Cole
A New Baby Is Coming to My House. Chihiro Iwasaki
Nobody Asked Me If I Wanted a Baby Sister. Martha Alexander
Our New Baby. Jane Hamilton-Merritt
Peter's Chair. Erza Jack Keats
Rabbit Inn. Patience Brewster
Spot's Baby Sister. Eric Hill
That New Baby. Sara Bonnett Stein
Waiting for Baby. Tom Birdseye
Waiting for Hannah. Marisabina Russo
We Got This New Baby at Our House. Janet Sinberg
Welcome, Little Baby. Aliki
We're Going to Have a Baby. Doris Helmering
When the New Baby Comes, I'm Moving Out. Martha Alexander
Whose Mouse Are You? Robert Kraus
You Were Born on Your First Birthday. Linda Walvoord Girard

❧ Appendix 2 ————————

Board Books

This list of selected board books can be given to parents, or used to check against your own library's collection.

All Fall Down. Helen Oxenbury
Animals at the Zoo. Kenneth Lilly
Animals in the Country. Kenneth Lilly
Animals in the Jungle. Kenneth Lilly
Animals of the Ocean. Kenneth Lilly
Animals on the Farm. Kenneth Lilly
Animal Sounds. Aurelius Battaglia
At My House. Margaret Miller
At Night. Anne Rockwell
At the Playground. Anne Rockwell
Bathtime for Mouse. Helmut Spanner
Clap Hands. Helen Oxenbury
Dressing. Helen Oxenbury
Family. Helen Oxenbury
Fat Mouse. Harry Stevens
A First Book in My Garden. Brimax
A First Book in My Kitchen. Brimax
A First Book in My Nursery. Brimax

A First Book in My Toybox. Brimax
Friends. Helen Oxenbury.
Gobble Growl Grunt. Peter Spier
Good Night Moon. Margaret Wise Brown
I'm a Baby. Phoebe Dunn
In My Room. Margaret Miller
In the Morning. Anne Rockwell
In the Rain. Anne Rockwell
Mouse Visits the Kitchen. Helmut Spanner
Me and My Clothes. Margaret Miller.
The Real Mother Goose Husky Book I. Blanche Fisher Wright
Say Goodnight. Helen Oxenbury
Teddy Bear Plays in the Water. Helmut Spanner
Teddy Bear's Day. Helmut Spanner
Tickle, Tickle. Helen Oxenbury
Time to Eat. Margaret Miller
What? Leo Lionni
When? Leo Lionni
Where? Leo Lionni
Who? Leo Lionni
Whose Baby Are You? Debby Slier
Working. Helen Oxenbury

✒ Appendix 3

Compact Discs for Programming

The following recordings are available on compact discs for those libraries that prefer that format for programming.

Adventures in Rhythm by Ella Jenkins
American Folk Songs for Children by Mike and Peggy Seeger
Animal Folk Songs for Children by Mike, Penny, and Peggy Seeger
Baby Beluga by Raffi
Babysong by Hap Palmer
Burl Ives Sings Little White Duck by Burl Ives
The Cat Came Back by Fred Penner
Corner Grocery Store by Raffi
Danny Kaye for Children by Danny Kaye
Evergreen, Everblue by Raffi
Everything Grows by Raffi
Fred Penner's Place by Fred Penner
Happy Birthday by Sharon, Lois and Bram
A House for Me by Fred Penner
Jump Children by Marcy Marxer
Kaddywompas by Tim Noah
Lullabies and Night Songs by Alex Wilder
Mail Myself to You by John McCutcheon

More Singable Songs by Raffi
My Street Begins at My House by Ella Jenkins
Nursery Days by Woody Guthrie
One Light, One Sun by Raffi
Pete Seeger Children's Concert at Town Hall by Pete Seeger
Peter, Paul and Mommy by Peter, Paul and Mary
Rise and Shine by Raffi
Sing from A to Z by Sharon, Lois and Bram
Singable Songs for the Very Young by Raffi
Songs to Grow On by Woody Guthrie
Walter the Waltzing Worm by Hap Palmer
When the Rain Comes Down by Cathy Fink
You'll Sing a Song and I'll Sing a Song by Ella Jenkins

Appendix 4

Selected Sources of Records, Tapes, and Films

Records and Tapes

ABC School Supply, Inc.
3312 N. Berkeley Lake Rd.
P.O. Box 100019
Duluth, GA 30136-9419

Childcraft
20 Kilmer Rd.
Edison, NJ 08818-3081

Chinaberry Book Service
2780 Via Orange Way,
  Suite B
Spring Valley, CA 91978

Constructive Playthings
1227 East 119th St.
Grandview, MO 64030

Educational Record Center
Building 400 / Suite 400
1575 Northside Dr. N.W.
Atlanta, GA 30318-4298

Educational Record and
  Tape Distributors
61 Bennington Ave.
Freeport, NY 11520

Kimbo Educational
Dept. M
P.O. Box 477
Long Branch, NJ 07740-
  0477

Music for Little People
P.O. Box 1460
1144 Redway Dr.
Redway, CA 95560

Films

Aims Media
6901 Woodley Ave.
Van Nuys, CA 91406-4878

Britannica Films
425 N. Michigan Ave.
Chicago, IL 60611

Campus Films
20 Overhill Rd.
Scarsdale, NY 10583

Churchill Films
12210 Nebraska Ave.
Los Angeles, CA 90025

Contemporary Films
McGraw Hill
110 15th St.
Del Mar, CA 92014

Coronet/MTI Film and
   Video
108 Wilmot Rd.
Deerfield, IL 60015

Cypress Films
P.O. Box 4872
Carmel, CA 93921

Direct Cinema
P.O. Box 69799
Los Angeles, CA 90069

International Film Bureau
332 S. Michigan Ave.
Chicago, IL 60604

Lekotek
613 Dempster St.
Evanston, IL 60201

Lucerne Films
37 Ground Pine Rd.
Morris Plains, NJ 07950

Paramount
   Communications
6912 Tujunga Ave.
North Hollywood, CA
   91605

Perspective Films
369 West Erie St.
Chicago, IL 60610

Phoenix Films
13-A Jules La.
New Brunswick, NJ 08901

Pyramid Films
Box 1048
Santa Monica, CA 90406

Walt Disney Films
See Coronet/MTI Film and
   Video

Weston Woods
Weston, CT 06883

❧ Appendix 5 ───────────

Toy Manufacturers and Sources

ABC School Supply Inc.
3312 N. Berkeley Lake Rd.
P.O. Box 100019
Duluth, GA 30136-9419

Animal Town
P.O. Box 7529
Healdsburg, CA 95448

Aristoplay
P.O. Box 7529
Ann Arbor, Mi 48107

The Ark Catalog
4245 Crestline Ave.
Fair Oaks, CA 95628

Battat Inc.
P.O. Box 1264
2 Industrial Blvd.
West Circle
Plattsburgh, NY 12901

Brio Scanditoy Corp.
6531 N. Sidney Place
Milwaukee, WI 53209

Childcraft
20 Kilmer Rd.
Edison, NJ 08818-3081

Child's Play
Ashworth Road, Bridgemead
Swindon SN 57YD
England

Community Playthings
Route 213
Rifton, NY 12471

Constructive Playthings
1227 East 119th St.
Grandview, MO 64030-1117

Discovery Toys, Inc.
Martinez, CA 94553

DLM
P.O. Box 4000
One DLM Park
Allen, TX 75002

Educational Strategies
1004 S. Baldwin Ave.
Arcadia, CA 91006

The Enchanted Doll House
Route 7
Manchester Center, VT
    05255-9984

Environments, Inc.
P.O. Box 1348
Beaufort, SC 29902

F.A.O. Schwarz
767 Fifth Ave.
New York, NY 10153

First Steps, Ltd.
Hand in Hand
Catalog Center
9180 LeSaint Dr.
Fairfield, OH 45014

Fisher-Price
620 Girard Ave.
East Aurora, NY 14052-1879

Galt Toys
James Galt and Co., Inc.
60 Church St.
Wallingford, CT 06492

The Gifted Children's Catalog
2922 N. 35th Ave., Suite 4
Phoenix, AZ 85061-1408

Growing Child
P.O. Box 620
Lafayette, IN 47902

Hearth Song
P.O. Box B
Sebastopol, CA 95473-0601

Johnson and Johnson
Baby Products Company
Grandview Rd.
Skillman, NJ 08558

Judy Instructo
4325 Hiawatha Ave. so.
Minneapolis, MN 55406

Just for Kids
75 Patterson St.
P.O. Box 15006
New Brunswick, NJ 08906-5006

Kapable Kids
P.O. Box 250
Bohemia, NY 11716

Kaplan Corp.
P.O. Box 609
Lewisville, NC 27023

Learn and Play
Troll Associates
100 Corporate Dr.
Mahwah, NJ 07498-1053

Lego Systems, Inc.
P.O. Box 640
Enfield, CT 06082

Metropolitan Museum of Art
    Catalog
Special Sales Department
P.O. Box 1044
Boston, MA 02120

Museum of Modern Art Catalog
Mail Order Department
11 West 53rd St.
New York, NY 10029

Play Fair Toys
1690 28th St.
Boulder, CO 80301

Play 'n Peace
P.O. Box 775
Medford, NJ 08055

The Right Start Catalog
Right Start Plaza
5334 Sterling Center Dr.
Westlake Village, CA 91361

Smithsonian Institution Catalog
P.O. Box 2456
Washington, DC 20013

Things from Bell
230 Mechanic St.
P.O. Box 206
Princeton, WI 54968

Toys for Special Children
101 Lefurgy Ave.
Hastings-On-Hudson, NY 10706

Toys for the Handicapped
76 Barracks Rd.
Sandy Lane Industrial Estate
Stourport-On-Severn
Worcestershire, DY 139QB
England

Oppenheim Toy Portfolio (A
    quarterly review)
40 E. 9th St.
New York, NY 10003
Annual subscription, 4 issues.

Toys to Grow On
P.O. Box 17
Long Beach, CA 90801

Playthings (A magazine)
Geyer-McAllister Publications,
    Inc.
51 Madison Ave.
New York, NY 10010
Annual subscription, 11 issues.

Playthings puts out a special 91–
92 issue titled *Who Makes It?*
which includes alphabetical
listings of manufacturers and
importers, sources classified by
categories, etc.

✒ Bibliographic Sources ───

Carlson, Ann D. *Early Childhood Literature Sharing Programs in Libraries*. Hamden, CT: Library Professional Publications/The Shoe String Press, 1985.

Caruso, David A. "Instant Exploratory Play." *Young Children* (November 1984).

Clark, Margaret M. *Young Fluent Readers: What Can They Teach Us?* London: Heinemann, 1976.

Field, Tiffany. "Baby Research Comes of Age." *Psychology Today* (May 1987).

──────. *Infancy*. Cambridge, MA: Harvard University Press, 1990.

"For Kid's Sake—Think Toy Safety." Washington, D.C.: U.S. Consumer Safety Commission (August 1987).

Hearne, Betsy. *Sharing Books with Young Children*. (video-cassette). Chicago: American Library Association, 1986.

Hektoen, Faith H. "The Connecticut Research Documentation Project." *School Library Journal* (April 1980).

Hirsch, Elizabeth. *The Block Book*. Washington, D.C.: National Association for the Education of Young Children, 1974.

"How to Be a Winner at Toy Buying." *Learning Magazine* (November 1977).

Huck, Charlotte S., Susan Ingrid Hepler, and Janet Hickman. *Children's Literature in the Elementary School, 4th Edition*. New York: Holt, Rinehart and Winston, 1987.

Keeshan, Robert. *Growing Up Happy: Captain Kangaroo Tells Yesterday's Children How to Nurture Their Own*. New York: Doubleday, 1989.

Lawson, Carol. "Who Believes in Make-Believe? Not the New Toys." *New York Times* (February 6, 1992).

Levin, Diane. "Today's TV Toys." *American Health* (December 1988).

MacDonald, Margaret Read. *Booksharing: 101 Programs to Use with Preschoolers*. Hamden, CT: Library Professional Publication/The Shoe String Press, 1988.

Markey, Judy. "Long Live the Little Red Wagon." *Woman's Day* (December 1, 1988).

Oppenheim, Joanne. *Buy Me! Buy Me!: The Bank Street Guide to Choosing Toys for Children*. New York: Pantheon, 1987.

Piers, Maria and Genevieve Millet Landau. *The Gift of Play*. New York: Walker and Company, 1980.

Renner, Gerard. "Warped Toys Debase Yule Spirit, Priest Says." *Hartford Courant* (December 2, 1990).

Schickebanz, Judith A. *More Than ABC's: The Early Stages of Reading and Writing*. Washington, D.C.: National Association for the Education of Young Children, 1986.

Self, Frank and Nancy DeSalvo. "List of Selected Toys for Children Under Three." Hartford: Connecticut State Library, 1984.

Smardo, Frances A. "Are Librarians Prepared to Serve Young Children?" *Journal of Education for Librarianship 20* (Spring 1980).

Stone, L. Joseph. *Childhood and Adolescence*. New York: Random House, 1978.

Taylor, Susan Champlin. "A Promise at Risk." *Modern Maturity*, (August–September, 1989).

"Toys = Tools for Learning." Washington, D.C.: National Association for the Education of Young Children, 1985.

White, Burton. "Baby Research Comes of Age." *Psychology Today* (May 1987).

White, Burton, and Michael K. Meyerhoff. "Making the Grade as Parents." *Psychology Today* (September 1986).

ᬐ Index to Toys ───────────

🐢 Index to Films ────────

Title Index to Records and Cassette Tapes

🎵 Author Index to Records and Cassette Tapes ————

🐢 Author-Title Index to Books and Articles

Kessler, Ethel, 77
Kessler, Leonard, 77
Komaiko, Leah, 98
Kraus, Robert, 45, 70, 142
Krauss, Ruth, 44, 68

Landau, Genevieve Miller, 147
Levin, Diane, 126
Levinson, Riki, 53
Levy, Elizabeth, 135
Levy, Janine, 16
Lilly, Kenneth, 29
Lindgren, Barbro, 45, 48, 142
Lionni, Leo, 35, 143
Little Fox Goes to the End of the World, 96
Lizzie and Harold, 99
"Long Live the Little Red Wagon," 122
Look, There's My Hat, 113

McCloskey, Robert, 143
McCully, Emily A., 112
Machines at Work, 113
MacDonald, Margaret Read, 39
The Magic Years, 135
Make Way for Ducklings, 143
"Making the Grade as Parents," 4
Markey, Judy, 122
Martin, Bill Jr., 75, 114, 143
Mary Wore Her Red Dress and Henry Wore His Green Sneakers, 114
Matterson, Elizabeth, 33
Mayer, Mercer, 48, 90, 111, 140
Mealtime, 92
Me and My Clothes, 33
Messy Baby, 33
Meyerhoff, Michael, 4
Mike Mulligan and His Steam Shovel, 95, 110, 113
Miller, Jane, 112
Miller, Margaret, 33, 113
Mr. Brown Can Moo, Can You?, 58
Misty's Mischief, 111
More, More, More, Said the Baby, 60
More Than ABC's: The Early Stages of Reading and Writing, 22
Morris, Ann, 92

The Most Amazing Hide-and-Seek Alphabet Book, 82
The Most Amazing Hide-and Seek Counting Book, 82
Mouse Paint, 114
Mouse Visits the Kitchen, 29
Munari, Bruno, 113, 143
My Brown Bear Barney, 93, 114
My Very First Book of Shapes, 80

The New Read-Aloud Handbook, 141
Newson, Elizabeth, 34
Newson, John, 34
Newton, Laura P., 113
Night Noises, 96
Noah and the Great Flood, 112
Noah's Ark, 112
Noisy, 45, 50
Number of Things, 4, 82

Of Colors and Things, 81
Oh Dear!, 54
Oh, No!, 44, 52
Old MacDonald Had a Farm, 74, 113
Old Mother Hubbard, 54
The Old Woman and Her Pig, 143
Oppenheim, Joanne, 126
Ormerod, Jan, 33, 113, 140
1,2,3 to the Zoo, 44, 50, 113
One Was Johnny, 61
Our Day, 44
Oxenbury, Helen, 26, 29, 33, 82

Pat-A-Cake, 44
Peek, Merle, 114
Peek-A-Boo!, 45, 48
Perkins, Al, 54, 143
Petersham, Maud, 74, 112, 144
Petersham, Miska, 74, 112, 144
Picnic, 112
Pierre, 80
Piers, Maria W., 147
Piggy at the Wheel, 114
Planes, 114
Playing, 29
The Plug-In Drug, 148
Poems of a Nonny Mouse, 92
Poulsson, Emilie, 16